CONTENTS

INTRODUCTION

It's sunrise on Williams Hill. From deep inside my sleeping bag, I emerge to look out over the glowing orange hills of Southern Illinois, and beyond, the Ohio River Valley. Out of my peripheral vision, I see something bright and shining. On the handlebars of my mountain bike, a drop of dew catches the sunlight as if to say, "Get up! It's time to ride!"

Suited up and ready, I have no inkling of what a sweet ride lies ahead. When your body feels strong, your bike is running smoothly, and it's 65 degrees in November, spectacular scenery is just icing on the cake. Indeed, icing is what I got.

From creek valley to hilltop glade, the Shawnee woods opened up to me, exposing secret deer licks and ancient native hideaways — there's evidence that Indians took refuge under rock overhangs in this area. This southern tip of the state escaped the ice sheet thousands of years ago; tremendous volumes of melt water helped sculpt its powerful, bizarre rock formations. It was my great fortune to be able to ride here: hugging the sides of hills, swooping down dry creek beds, working my way up to overlooks, and stopping regularly to admire the amazing rocks.

A mountain bike lets you explore almost the same country you could see on foot, but cover far more terrain in a day.

What better way to appreciate America's vast stretches of backcountry public lands up close?

This reminded me of what I love about mountain biking: What better way to see the outdoors? Although I dearly love hiking, on foot I would only have seen a portion of the country I covered easily on my bike in one afternoon. Motorized vehicles are rightly prohibited from the narrow forest trails. Only on a mountain bike can you traverse terrain in this way, close enough to see a woodpecker, fast enough to cover 20 miles before dinner. To me, the mountain bike is the perfect vehicle for exploration.

I came to mountain biking gently, tentatively. While living in my first home after college, I could hit a trail from my apartment's back door that led to an extensive, intertwining network of paths on a nearby wooded college campus. Exploring the rolling, meandering dirt trails was a pleasant way to spend evenings after work. At the time, I had no dreams of tackling big mountains or rocky hillsides. I just liked the fact that I could pedal and see raccoons and field mice, black-eyed Susans and wild strawberries, all less than a mile from my suburban home. Though my mountain bike, with its upright handlebars and knobby tires, had transported me around town and school for years, this was my first off-road experience. Before long, I grew addicted to pedaling through the woods.

Over the next few years, I began attempting longer, more challenging trails with my boyfriend, and questions occurred to me: Why were my fingers sometimes numb after a long ride, even in warm weather? Where could I find a helmet that didn't constantly fall into my eyes because it was too big? And the big one: Where were all the other women mountain bikers and how could I meet them?

On cold winter days, suffering mountain biking withdrawal, I devoured all the bike magazines I could read. I visited bike shops, studied books about bike maintenance, and took a closer look at my bike. I washed off the dried mud, lubricated my neglected chain, tried truing my wheels, and took a few things apart that I shouldn't have. More questions occurred to me: What would I do if I got a flat tire and became stranded alone on a trail? Would I — a 110-pound rider — really benefit from the added weight of a suspension fork? A suspension seat post? A full suspension bike? Was I getting my money's worth from the mechanics at the bike shop, who sometimes didn't even seem to take me seriously, or would I be better off working on my own bike? Every day brought more questions: What's the difference between men's and women's bike shorts and saddles? What does a saddle sore look like? How do I deal with this darn poison ivy?

While bike magazines and the mostly male bike shop employees were of some help, it was only when I began to meet, talk to, and ride with other women mountain bikers that I learned everything I needed to know.

This book brings together the stories, advice, and sometimes mistakes of women of all ages and abilities who share a love of mountain biking. These women — bike industry experts, professional racers, and casual riders — will help answer your particular questions so you can have more fun on your mountain bike.

Enjoy the ride!

GEARING UP

When buying a mountain bike, most people have in mind a specific use. They want to pedal a nearby city bike path on weekends with their children. They want to explore some rugged mountain trails with a friend who rides. They want to start biking to work for exercise (and because the parking fees are getting outrageous). They want to ride along the Continental Divide Trail to celebrate their 50th birthday.

Think long and hard about how you plan to use your bike. Where do you expect to ride and on what kind of terrain? Do you plan to ride rocky single-track trails or gravel fire roads?

What kind of rider are you now? Are you the daredevil type who's the first to take risks, or do you prefer to go the slower and safer route? How often do you expect to ride your new bike? How long do you expect to be in the saddle on a typical ride? Think big ("I want to win the Women's Sport category races in the local mountain bike race series"), but also think realistically ("I will probably ride to work occasionally in good weather and ride off-road trails a couple of weekends a month"). The more you have thought about the type of riding you plan or expect to do, the easier the job of choosing the right bike will be.

Perfect conditions along the White Rim Trail, Canyonlands National Park, Utah.

equipment stores rent mountain bikes by the hour or day. Some bike shops allow customers to borrow demonstration bikes. Ride as many bikes as possible with different types of frames and components. Ride a bike with twist shifters and one with thumb shifters. Ride an aluminum frame bike and a cro-moly frame bike. Ride bikes with and without suspension. If you're sure you'll never venture out to rough trails, ride a hybrid bike, which has thinner tires and upright handlebars.

Test Ride Bikes

The next step in finding the right bike is to ride a few. Borrow a bike from a friend who's your size and pedal it around on the type of terrain you expect to ride. Rent a bike, or two, or three. Many bike shops, resorts, and outdoor

Some people will throw down $800 for the first bike they ride around the bike store's parking lot, but there are better ways to ensure you're getting the bike that will make you happy.

Read About Bikes

When purchasing a car you might peruse *Consumer Reports* or *Car and Driver*. Likewise, you may want to read several bicycle magazines before shopping for your bike. *Bicycling, Mountain Bike, Bike, Mountain Biker,* and *Dirt Rag* are some publications which offer essential information about bike models currently on the market. Staff at these magazines test ride and review hot new bikes and products

Evening light on a back road near Stowe, Vermont. Mountain biking is more than single-track riding in the mountains.

every month. *Caution: Some of these magazines are geared exclusively toward 25-year-old men who like to race down rocky hillsides.* Don't let these magazines' marketing strategies put you off. They're full of good information and you'll learn a lot about bikes and mountain biking if you can get past this male bias. Also, be forewarned that many of the bikes reviewed are top-of-the-line, super-expensive models with fancy high-tech hardware that few beginners need.

Several of the aforementioned magazines publish annual bike

review issues at the end of the year, in which bikes on the market are categorized according to price and type of bike. These special issues provide information about different manufacturers' bikes at a glance — sizes available, component specifications, frame materials, bike weight — and can be very helpful for narrowing down your choices. However, they may neglect to include some of the small, independent manufacturers who make bikes with smaller frame sizes designed for a woman's proportions. That's where manufacturers' catalogs come in.

Most bike manufacturers offer promotional catalogs that contain specific information, such as the bikes' size range, type of components, frame materials, frame geometry and measurements, and other specifications. Two important specifications that these catalogs usually omit are bike weight and price. Turn to reputable bike shops for answers. If you're having trouble tracking down a particular manufacturer's catalog, ask at a bike shop for the manufacturer's address or phone number so you can order a catalog. Or turn to "Sources & Resources" at the back of this book for details.

The Internet is also a good source of current information about bikes. Most of the major bike magazines and manufacturers offer Web sites with product information. Some Web sites, such as www.mtbr.com, contain independent product reviews by individuals who own the equipment reviewed and can attest to its strengths and weaknesses.

Have Fun

Looking at all the cool bikes on the market, narrowing down your choices, and finally buying the right bike can be a satisfying experience. If it's been a while since you've had a bike, you'll be amazed at the technology bike manufacturers use these days. Have a good time and don't allow yourself to get too overwhelmed by all the choices.

FINDING A WOMAN-FRIENDLY BIKE SHOP

When Michele Keane of Edwards, Colorado, began to visit local shops in search of her first mountain bike, she frequently got the cold shoulder from the mostly male staffers.

"I felt intimidated to begin with and their snooty attitude didn't make me feel any better," Keane said. "It made me dread going into bike shops, which was a drag because that's one of the best ways to learn about bikes and riding."

Several years later, after Keane had become a Top 20 pro racer, she got the royal treatment. "All of a sudden, I was the queen. Everybody wanted to help me. It made me mad.

A monumental cactus, Saguaro National Monument, near Tucson, Arizona.

I mean, where were they when I really needed help?"

This section is dedicated to all the women who have received poor service in a bike store. It happens. Sometimes you run into a shop where the staff treats you rudely, ignores you, talks down to you, or jumps to conclusions about your riding habits based on your gender or appearance. The employees may be having a bad day, are really busy, or simply don't have a clue how to serve women. Sometimes you enter a store feeling overwhelmed by all the stuff you don't know and leave feeling even worse because of a bad employee. In any case, don't let it discourage you. You don't have to put up with poor service.

Believe me, there are many more good people and bike shops out there than bad. A good salesperson will make you feel welcome, answer your questions in terms you understand, anticipate questions you may not have thought of, and help you find what you're looking for (even if it means ordering an item not in stock).

Bike shops develop reputations. Ask other women who ride which shops they like and why. Ask a friend who's an experienced mountain biker to go bike shopping with you. Check the Internet for local bike club Web sites. Women club members may be able to steer you to some good shops. Visit as many bike stores as you can. First impressions are valuable. If a

shop is well lighted and clean, and seems to have a good selection of women's clothing, it is making an effort to serve the women who come through its doors. If you live in a metropolitan area or a town with several bike shops, consider yourself lucky. If you do happen on a store whose staff treats you like you're invisible, you have the luxury of blowing them off and going to another store. For the best service, avoid bike shops at busy or inopportune times like weekends, big sales, and right before closing time. Look for a bike shop that employs women. A woman salesperson can convey a sensitivity to your needs that will prove invaluable.

Ask lots of questions. Voice your concerns. Be polite, but straightforward. Don't be shy about getting the information you need. The only way to get good service is to let a salesperson know what you need. For example: "Could you please explain this bike's shifting system in layman's terms?" or "I know you say this bike is the right size for me, but my neck and shoulders feel strained when I'm riding."

Once you find a store that you like, stop in regularly, even if you don't make a purchase every time. Quality bike shops are a mountain biker's best friend. Why? They're fun to visit and they're an essential source of information about local trails, bargains on bikes and accessories, advice on maintaining and

Fine-tuning saddle height (left) and questioning the width of the handlebars (right). Search for a woman-friendly bike shop where your concerns are taken seriously.

repairing your bike, and finding other people to ride with. At a good bike store you can learn when the next volunteer trail work day is, where to register for the local fat tire festival, and why your bike's shifting has become sluggish. A good bike mechanic is equally valuable, especially if you've just started mountain biking. Your previous mechanical experience may be limited and you may need several adjustments to your bike to make it fit correctly. (By the way, don't expect to find this service or information at a department or discount store. The guy in the sporting goods department at Super-Buys who sells you a bike today may have been working in the pet depart-

ment selling hamsters yesterday.)

If you've tried the local shops and just aren't satisfied with the service or products offered, try mail order. A lot of women rely on catalog shopping for bikes, clothing, and accessory purchases for good reason. There are some excellent mail-order companies that sell biking products designed especially for women. (See "Sources & Resources" for names and phone numbers.) Many are small businesses staffed by other women cyclists who know what you're going through because they've been through it too. But even if you buy all your gear through mail-order catalogs, it pays to visit a bike shop from time to time.

WHAT YOU GET WHEN YOU PAY MORE

Two factors determine a bicycle's cost: the material the bike's frame is made of and the type of compo- nents, or parts, that come on the bike. In general, the lighter a bike's frame and components, the more expensive. When you pay more for a bike, you should also be getting

WOMEN'S MOUNTAIN BIKE ANATOMY

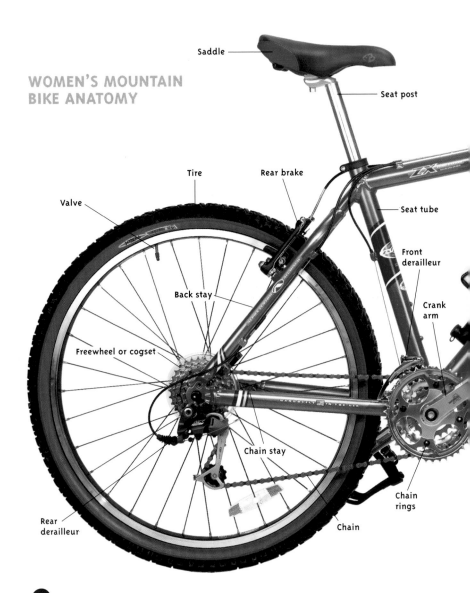

Saddle

Seat post

Tire

Rear brake

Valve

Seat tube

Front derailleur

Back stay

Crank arm

Freewheel or cogset

Chain stay

Chain rings

Rear derailleur

Chain

more durable components. A lightweight, durable bike is very advantageous for a mountain biker who plans to ride off-road, particularly a woman, who is likely to be smaller, lighter, and weaker than a man. The lighter the bike, the easier it is to ride up hills, manuever through technical sections, and carry when it's necessary. A heavy bike wears

Bar end

Handlebar

Gear shifter

Brake lever

Stem

Top tube

Head tube

Down tube

Water bottle

Front brake

Front suspension

Tire pump

Toe clip

Fork blade

Rim

Pedal

you out faster and makes you dread those hills, while a lightweight, responsive bike can help you climb like a goat and feel like riding all day long.

Most women cyclists agree that female mountain bikers should be concerned about their bike's weight. Most bikes are designed for a 170-pound man, but the average woman weighs anywhere from 30 to 75 pounds less than the average man. She is also typically less strong. According to Christine Wells, author of *Women, Sport, and Performance:*

A Physiological Perspective, the average woman has just 56 percent of the upper-body strength of the average man and about 72 percent of his leg and hip strength. For these reasons, I recommend that women who plan to ride off-road trails look at bikes weighing 27 pounds or less; the lighter the better.

There are exceptions to this rule, however. If you expect to ride most of your miles on paved roads, gravel roads, or gentle trails, a very lightweight bike may not be as important. If you plan to use your

GEAR TALK
MORE FOR YOUR MONEY — BIKES NOW AND THEN

Ask a long-time mountain biker and she'll likely tell you how much better today's bikes are than the bikes of several years ago. Today, frames are lighter, brakes work better, and suspension systems are nothing short of amazing. That's good news for you, the consumer.

According to Vernon Felton, associate editor of *Mountain Biker* magazine, in 1983, a first-generation Specialized StumpJumper had a double-butted, chro-moly rigid steel frame, a 15-speed drivetrain, a weight of 31 pounds, 4 ounces, and a price of $775. Just five years later, the 1988 model StumpJumper had lost nearly three pounds in weight, gained three speeds in gearing, and remained the same in price. By 1998, the StumpJumper sported a lighter frame, direct-pull brakes, front suspension fork, clipless pedals, and 24 speeds. Its overall weight had dropped to 26 pounds. and its price had only increased by $324.

After adjusting the 1998 price for inflation, it's clear that you get more bike for your buck now than ever before. The market is constantly changing and high-tech parts trickle down to the masses quickly. So don't despair if you can't afford a bike with all the nicest parts now. If history is a guide, you might be able to afford one sooner than you think.

mountain bike to ride exclusively down hills, weight is not an issue. (Ski resorts cater to just such riders in the off season, with lifts that carry you to the tops of mountains so you can ride down without breaking a sweat.) Many mountain bikers also believe that the advantages of a full suspension bike — a more comfortable, less fatiguing ride — are well worth the few extra pounds these bikes sometimes weigh.

Overall, I am a strong believer in lightweight mountain bikes for women. A good, lightweight mountain bike is a pleasure to ride and will provide you with fun, healthy recreation and transportation for years to come.

THE FRAME

The frame forms the skeleton of a bike, to which its components, or parts, are attached. A traditional "diamond" style bike frame consists of a series of tubes — the top tube, head tube, down tube, seat tube, chain stay, and seat stay — configured in a diamond shape to suit a particular riding style. Qualities to look for in a bike frame include light weight, strength, and responsiveness. Most bike frames sold in reputable bike shops come with a lifetime guarantee. Bike frames are made out of a number of different materials that can affect a bike's weight, strength, ride quality, and price.

Frame Materials

HIGH-TENSILE STEEL Made of thick-walled, straight-gauge steel tubing, high-tensile steel bikes are the cheapies ($200 and under) you see lined up in the sporting goods sections of discount stores. While they might seem like a bargain, buyer beware — these heavy, lazy beasts would rather sit in your garage collecting dust and cobwebs than ride down (or, heaven forbid, up) a trail.

You might think that a bike as heavy as 32 pounds would at least be strong and durable. Not so. A friend who worked in a bike shop used to keep a high-tensile steel bike close at hand to dissuade that customer who inevitably asked, "What's so much better about a $300 bike than the one I saw at X-mart for $189?" Gleeful at the chance to demonstrate, Mike would make his point with brute force. One foot placed firmly on the heavy bike's top tube, he would bend the frame into a slight V, and then, smug and satisfied, sell the customer the $300 bike.

In short, I don't recommend buying a high-tensile steel bike. CHRO-MOLY STEEL Chro-moly, short for chrome molybdenum, is a steel alloy that comes in many strengths, weights, and thicknesses. Chro-moly tubing is made lightweight and strong using a process called "butting." A butted frame tube is thinner at the center and thicker at the ends to provide strength where it is most needed. Frame tubing can be double- or triple-butted to save weight without giving up strength. Chro-moly frames can be repaired fairly easily by an experienced frame technician. Chro-moly bikes range in price from $200 to $1000, depending on the quality of frame and components.

Because of the inherent shock-absorbing qualities of this frame material, a chro-moly bike feels resilient and forgiving. Rather than transmitting the vibrations from every tiny pebble you ride over straight to your body, the bike's frame absorbs some of the shock, which can make for a slightly more comfortable and less tiring ride. Jeremy Fields, an expert mountain bike racer and bike shop manager, recommends lightweight chro-moly bikes for women mountain bikers, particularly if they are small in stature.

"A lightweight [chro-moly] steel bike is an excellent choice for smaller riders because it stays very resilient and comfortable, even in smaller frame sizes," Fields says.

LADIES' FRAME BIKES

Perhaps the last bike you owned had a ladies' style frame, with a drastically sloping top tube. You may have noticed that the ladies' frame (also called step-through or mixte) has gone out of fashion. While it could be argued that this frame style has a few advantages for casual, around town riding or bike commuting (easier to mount and dismount, can be ridden while wearing a skirt), it has no place on a trail. The diamond frame with a horizontal top tube is much more efficient, strong, and better handling. If you plan to ride your mountain bike off-road or if you value responsive handling, don't get a ladies' frame bike.

ALUMINUM Aluminum frames generally weigh less than all but the most expensive chro-moly frames. They come in various tube thicknesses and some manufacturers (the best-known is Cannondale) make use of large-diameter, thin-walled aluminum tubing to produce a very light, strong, durable frame. Aluminum frame bikes range in price from $600 to $1500.

Mountain bikers describe aluminum frames as easy to handle, stable, efficient, and stiff. All of a rider's power is transferred directly through the stiff frame to the drivetrain, making for a quick, responsive bike. However, this quality also means that the frame transmits, rather than absorbs, the shock from bumps.

Margo Carroll, former pro mountain bike racer and now a freelance bike photographer, swears by her aluminum mountain bike. But it wasn't always that way. When Carroll began racing mountain bikes in 1990, it was on a chro-moly frame bike.

"Everybody had chro-moly bikes back then," she says. "But there also weren't many people using front suspension, so you really needed the flex of a chro-moly frame. With aluminum, your energy goes straight to moving the back wheel. It's very efficient. Sure, you feel the bumps more, but you can compensate by using a suspension fork."

While many women mountain bikers love aluminum frames, they have one disadvantage. When aluminum bike frames get smaller, the frame tubes become shorter and stiffer, resulting in an even harsher ride. Long rides on a small, unsuspended aluminum bike can be uncomfortable. I know. I rode a 14-inch Cannondale M500 mountain bike for three years without front or rear suspension. I now ride the same bike with seat post and front-end suspension and I love it. A quality saddle and lower tire pressure can also make the ride on a small aluminum bike more comfortable.

CARBON OR COMPOSITE FIBER
Some of the lightest bikes on the market today are made of carbon fiber, a relatively new material also known as thermoplastic or composite fiber. The carbon fiber frames manufactured today — made from layers of synthetic fibers and hard epoxy resin — are strong, durable, and dependable. Carbon fiber is one of the most shock-absorbing frame materials around, and riders sometimes describe the ride quality as forgiving or springy. However, carbon fiber bikes are expensive, starting at no less than $1000.

Big, burly, super-aggressive bikers (usually male) sometimes break carbon fiber frames. While these frames are anything but delicate, hard-core hell-on-wheels cyclists — especially those weighing more than 170 pounds — have been known to push them beyond their limits until they crack.

But carbon fiber can be an

excellent frame material for women and lighter male riders. Manufacturers Trek and Kestrel each make a carbon fiber mountain bike weighing around 22 pounds. Such ultra-light weight gives a mountain biker a significant advantage when climbing hills. It also helps conserve energy on long rides. An additional advantage to small carbon fiber frames is that as the bike's frame gets smaller, it gets stronger. And women tend to employ a less aggressive riding style than men do, so cracking is not an issue.

One caveat: Only a few manufacturers make carbon fiber frames these days so women under 5 feet, 3 inches have limited options for finding small-sized frames. Trek and Kestrel carbon fiber bikes tend to run long in the frame's top tube, which makes for an ill-fitting bike if you're small or short in the torso.

TITANIUM Titanium frames are the ultimate in light weight, strength, comfort, and efficiency. They are also the ultimate in price, with frames alone going for $1000 and up. Titanium has been used for years, primarily in the manufacture of military aircraft, because of its combination of strength and light weight. Mountain bikers lucky enough to have ridden a titanium bike say it combines the best ride qualities of chro-moly steel — resiliency, comfort — and aluminum — light weight, stiffness — without the disadvantages of either. Since there are only a small number

of titanium frame builders around, finding one that fits properly might be a challenge for some women. Litespeed and Alpine Designs each make a titanium mountain bike that is well designed for women. If you have a couple thousand dollars to shell out for a titanium bike, you might just be able to scrape together a few hundred extra for a custom-built frame designed to fit your body precisely.

BIKE FIT

Consider the following facts: (1) Most bikes made by major manufacturers are designed with a 170-pound rider in mind. (2) Most women don't weigh 170 pounds (3) Most bike frame geometries are designed according to a man's proportions. (4) Women generally are shorter than men, with shorter torso and arms, narrower shoulders, wider hips, and smaller hands.

According to Georgena Terry, founder and CEO of Terry Precision Cycling for Women, when women ride bicycles that were designed for men, they commonly feel discomfort in the neck, lower back, shoulders, crotch, hands, or wrists. Why? The frame's top tube may be too long, the handlebars too wide, the saddle too narrow or long, or the brake levers too far from the handlebars. I point this out not to discourage women from buying or riding bicycles. I say it to emphasize the care with which a woman should select her bike.

If you know what to look for and

are willing to take your time to get it right, you'll be rewarded with a great fit on a comfortable bike that you'll enjoy for a long time.

The first test of whether a bike is anywhere close to the right size is standover clearance. It is the distance between your crotch and the bike's top tube measured while you straddle the bike with your feet flat on the floor. A mountain bike that will be ridden off-road should have three to four inches of standover clearance. You can get by with less if you plan to ride primarily gentle paved trails or streets.

The author tries on a bike. At 5 feet, 1 inch tall, 110 pounds and with a short torso, she has difficulty finding the right fit.

Reach

One of the most common bike fit problems for a woman is that the frame's top tube is too long for her proportionally shorter torso, compared to a man's. This is true even for taller women. A too-long top tube can make you feel uncomfortably stretched out while gripping the handlebars. When fitting a bike, your upper body should feel relaxed, not cramped and not stretched. You should notice a slight bend in your elbows while riding. Some women believe that reach, even more than standover clearance, is the most important consideration when properly fitting a woman to a bike.

"Women are proportioned so differently than men, with longer legs and shorter torsos, that even though your legs may tell you to get a larger frame, if you listen, your torso may tell you something else," Carroll says. "Make sure the bike fits your upper body. You don't want to be too stretched out."

You can make several alterations to a bike with a slightly lengthy top tube. One solution is to buy a shorter handlebar stem or one with a slight "rise," which angles it upward. Be aware, however, that a stem with more rise will make the bike handle differently. Another option is to move your saddle forward slightly (no more than an inch). This adjustment is called "seat fore/aft." Carroll cautions against making radical changes in seat fore/aft as it can mess up the critical relationship between your saddle and pedal position and affect the bike's handling.

I experienced the "too stretched out" sensation, but it took me a while to figure it out. I would enjoy long rides, but the following day and for several days thereafter, I would have muscle spasms in my shoulders and under my arms. Moving my saddle forward about an inch solved the problem.

Take your time when checking to see if a bike fits. If your bike feels slightly uncomfortable now, it will feel worse on a long ride. Shop around and test ride as many bikes as you can to get a feel for different fits. Be aware that some bike shops may try to sell you a bike they have on the floor that comes closest in size. Don't be pushed into a purchase you're not completely satisfied with. Isabel Dickson, a mountain bike instructor at Nantahala Outdoor Center in Bryson City, North Carolina, cautions women to watch out for bike shops trying to unload their overstock bikes, especially at the end of the year.

"It's possible to get a good deal on a bike that way, but only if the bike fits you well. If not, it's a bad buy," Dickson says.

If your local bike shop doesn't have your size, ask if they can order it. A good bike shop will be able to adjust an almost-right bike so it fits you better. Check bike manufacturers' catalogs. Some manufacturers will ship a test bike to a shop for you to try out.

Although it may take some looking, rest assured that there is a bike out there to fit you. If I can find a good fit on a bike (I'm 5 feet, 1 inch, 110 pounds with a short torso, small hands, and long legs), I'm confident that you can too. Major bike manufacturers such as Trek and GT are finally beginning to respond to dealer and customer demand for

Make sure your bike fits your upper body. You don't want to be too stretched out.

better fitting bikes for women by offering models designed according to our proportions. Bicycles designed specifically for women may have smaller frames, shorter top tubes, softer suspension forks, smaller diameter grips, narrower handlebars, and slightly wider saddles. The steeper seat tube on Trek's Women's Specific Design mountain bikes places your hips over the cranks for more power and comfort, and a reduced head angle keeps your center of gravity forward for greater stability. Shorter top tubes and higher head tubes let you reach the handlebars while keeping your arms at a relaxed angle. The higher stem on some of these bikes also accommodates shorter arms and torsos, but may compromise good handling on tight, rugged, or hilly trails. A high stem provides less leverage for lifting the front end of the bike and can make steep climbs more difficult. At the end of this book is a list of manufacturers making bikes that fit women well.

COMPONENTS

A bike's components are its shifters, brakes, and gearing system. Components are priced according to their weight, durability, and functionality. Lightweight, durable components are important if you plan to ride your mountain bike off-road regularly. Components can be upgraded as you desire, making it possible to have a "whole new bike" by periodi-cally buying and installing better-functioning, more durable, and lighter weight components.

Note: If you find a bike that fits well, but you want a few different components, ask your bike sales-person if you can trade or pay the difference for parts such as clipless pedals, a shorter stem, or direct-pull brakes. Many times, they will let you.

Wheels

Though they may look delicate, a bike's wheels can sustain forces many times the bike's weight. You'll be astonished at the abuse your bicycle's wheels can withstand during the course of a mountain bike ride. The wheels consist of hubs, spokes, and rims. Look for aluminum alloy rims and stainless steel spokes for

■

IS CUSTOM THE ANSWER?

If you're serious about getting a bike that fits you well, yet you're having a hard time finding one, consider a custom-built bike. Although it's possible to pay as much as $2000 for a bike made from an exotic frame material like titanium, steel and aluminum custom bikes can be priced comparably to production ones. And even if you pay more for custom, you'll be glad you

did. A superior-fitting bike makes a big difference in your comfort and performance on the trail. You want to be pleased with your bike's comfort and handling in the future, so don't settle for a mediocre fit just because you want a bike NOW and don't want to wait. Several companies that make custom bikes for women include Fat City Cycles, Independent Fabrications, and Terry Precision Cycling for Women. See "Sources & Resources" for details.

Cantilever brakes (left) were common on mountain bikes until direct-pull brakes (right) were introduced several years ago. Direct-pulls produce better stopping power while requiring less effort, a boon to women with small hands.

strength, durability, light weight, and good stopping power in wet conditions. Upgrading later to a set of even lighter wheels can shave as much as a pound or more off the weight of your bike.

Brakes

Mountain bikes come with brakes in one of three styles: direct-pull or "V-brakes," cantilever brakes, and disc brakes. While cantilever brakes were the standard for years, most mountain bikes priced over $300 now come with direct-pull brakes. Women cyclists especially benefit from this change in technology, since direct-pulls offer better stopping power while requiring less hand strength to squeeze the brake levers. Direct-pull brakes are also easier to adjust than cantilevers at the crucial brake pad/rim contact point.

Some expensive mountain bikes — especially those made just for downhilling — now come with hydraulic disc brakes. With traditional rim brakes, squeezing the brake lever pulls the brake cable, activating the brake caliper. The caliper grips both sides of the wheel rim to stop the wheel. Disc brakes, on the other hand, use the same technology as motorcycle brakes. Squeezing the brake levers pumps fluid to the brake caliper, which grips a disc mounted to the wheel's hub, rather than gripping its rim. Disc brakes provide certain advantages for mountain biking: They don't lose stopping power when wet as rim brakes do, they don't damage

Brake levers typically come adjusted to mens' large hands. Ask your bike shop mechanic to adjust yours so that you can comfortably reach them.

27 gears — most of them very low — to allow you to climb steep hills and ride over obstacles. The gears are divided between three chain rings in the front and seven, eight, or nine cogs in the back. The shifters on your handlebars are connected to the front and rear derailleurs via a cable, allowing you to change gears. Sometimes beginners are confused about gearing: when to use certain gears and how to shift properly. We'll talk more about shifting gears in Chapter 4 — Learning to Ride Off-Road.

your rims in gritty conditions, and the brake pads last much longer than rim brake pads. However, they currently cost and weigh twice as much as (or more than) rim brakes.

Drivetrain

The drivetrain, which transfers power from your leg muscles to turn the pedals and propel the bike, consists of the crankset, the pedals, the freewheel or cogset, the chain, and the front and rear derailleurs.

Mountain bikes have 21, 24, or

PEDALS The idea of having one's feet bound to the pedals intimidates some women. After riding bikes with standard platform pedals and sneakers your whole life, being attached to a bike by your feet can be scary. However, there are significant advantages to using some sort of foot-

GEAR TALK

BRAKE LEVERS

A woman's hands are typically smaller than a man's, making for an uncomfortable stretch from the handlebars to the brake levers on many bikes. If you can't squeeze your brake levers without straining, ask your bike mechanic to adjust the levers to bring them closer to the handlebars.

binding pedal system for off-road riding and it doesn't take long to get used to.

Having your feet bound to the pedals prevents them from bouncing off on rough sections of trail and improves the efficiency of each pedal stroke. The two types of foot binding used by mountain bikers are toe clips and clipless pedals.

A toe clip is a semi-flexible plastic cage with a nylon mesh cinch strap to keep the foot attached firmly to a regular platform pedal. Beginners usually keep the straps fairly loose so they can insert and remove their feet easily while they learn. Toe clips should not feel tight. Leave enough slack in the cinch strap to get your foot in and out freely, but not so much that your feet flop around inside the cage. Toe

Standard handlebars can be too wide for a woman's narrow shoulders. Consider asking your bike dealer to cut them down for you.

clips are inexpensive and preferred by people who don't want to buy special shoes for biking or who feel

FRAME GEOMETRY AND HOW YOU RIDE

When looking at mountain bikes in a bike shop, you may have noticed that a $700 bike looks different than a $300 one. The $700 bike looks racier . . . faster somehow, and it's not just the flashy paint job. The $300 bike — designed to appeal to the casual rider concerned primarily with comfort — has a different frame geometry than the $700

bike, which was designed for a performance-minded rider.

Frame geometry refers to the measurement of the angles on a bike frame between the top tube, seat tube, down tube, and head tube. Frame geometries on $300 bikes generally accommodate a relaxed, casual riding style. The steering is a little slower, resulting in a stable, predictable ride. The rider usually sits upright as a

continued on page 32

continued from page 31

result of a stem that angles upward. Be aware that this upright riding position puts more pressure on your butt, making a well padded saddle important for comfort. This type of frame geometry is appropriate for riding on streets, paved bike paths, and very easy off-road trails.

The $700 bike looks faster because it is designed to be ridden faster and more aggressively. Performance or race geometry — with a steeper head tube angle and a shorter wheel base — means quicker steering for negotiating tight turns and more efficient transfer of power from the pedals to the drivetrain. It means the rider generally leans over the handlebars in a more aggressive position, essential if she's finessing her way through a rough section of singletrack. These bikes are designed so that the rider's weight is (ideally) distributed evenly among three pressure points: hands on handlebars, feet on pedals, and butt on saddle.

Which type of frame geometry you choose should depend on how you prefer to ride.

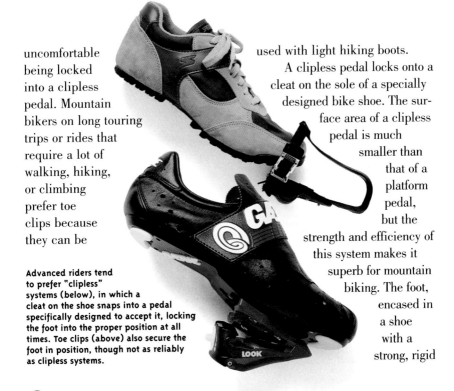

uncomfortable being locked into a clipless pedal. Mountain bikers on long touring trips or rides that require a lot of walking, hiking, or climbing prefer toe clips because they can be used with light hiking boots.

A clipless pedal locks onto a cleat on the sole of a specially designed bike shoe. The surface area of a clipless pedal is much smaller than that of a platform pedal, but the strength and efficiency of this system makes it superb for mountain biking. The foot, encased in a shoe with a strong, rigid

Advanced riders tend to prefer "clipless" systems (below), in which a cleat on the shoe snaps into a pedal specifically designed to accept it, locking the foot into the proper position at all times. Toe clips (above) also secure the foot in position, though not as reliably as clipless systems.

sole, is attached directly to the bike's crankarm, creating a powerful piston for climbing hills and manuevering over technical terrain. A twist of the ankle frees the foot from the pedal quickly. This pedal-binding system is preferred by performance

The efficiency of the clipless pedal system makes it ideal for mountain biking, provided you don't intend to combine much hiking with your riding.

mountain bikers and racers. Clipless pedals can be purchased as an upgrade for $60 to $130.

While many beginning mountain bikers follow a progression from platform pedals to toe clips to clipless pedals, mountain bike instructor Isabel Dickson suggests skipping the toe clip stage.

"I recommend that beginners get comfortable with their bikes by riding on gentle trails and forest roads using regular platform pedals. Once they are feeling confident, they should go straight to clipless pedals. Removing your foot from a toe clip is not a natural motion. It involves pulling your foot back and out of the cage. Clipless pedals, on the other hand, are much more similar to platform pedals; just a twist and your foot is off the pedal. Beginners should set

their clipless pedals super-loose and grease them every time they ride so their feet are easily freed," Dickson says.

Both pedal systems require some getting used to, and it's smart to practice on smooth, flat terrain while you become accustomed to the motion of inserting and removing your foot from the binding.

Shifters

Two different types of shifters are generally available on new mountain bikes: twist shifters, which operate with a twist of the hand on the grips, and trigger shifters, which operate using the thumb and index finger to click the shifter's buttons. Twist and trigger shifters are indexed, which means they click into a higher or lower gear with a twist of your hand

An indexed click gear shifter integrated into the grip and brake lever.

Handlebars

A woman's shoulders are generally narrower than a man's. As a result, a bike's handlebars may be too wide for her, causing aching shoulders and neck. If you feel this might be the case, a bike mechanic can cut your handlebars down. However, make sure he or she doesn't cut more than an inch off each end or you could lose steering control.

Suspension

FRONT SUSPENSION Back in the early nineties when Margo Carroll began racing mountain bikes, very few Midwestern racers used suspension forks. So when Carroll bought one of the first RockShox suspension forks and put it on her bike, she got some teasing from fellow bikers who thought she was succumbing to high-tech snake oil. Not long afterward, she started winning every race she entered by three minutes. The teasing stopped and local racers started buying suspension forks in droves.

newer models are much easier to use.

or the push of a button. Each type of shifter has its merits and disadvantages; preference for a certain type of shifter is personal.

When I bought my mountain bike five years ago, it came with twist shifters, an idea that appealed to me at first because of the fact that I would never have to remove so much as a finger from the handlebar grips to shift gears. In practice, however, I found that my shifters required considerable force to twist, making me less likely to change gears as often as I should and causing my hands to be sore at the end of a long ride. I finally replaced my twist shifters with a set of old-style, above the handlebar thumb shifters and have used them succesfully ever since. However, many women love twist shifters and don't have any trouble at all, and

Carroll believes strongly that a suspension fork has the potential to make a mountain biker ride better, faster, and more comfortably, no matter what her skill level. Why? Instead of bouncing off every rock and root it comes into contact with, the bike's front end rolls easily over these obstacles. Rather than feeling like you've been jackhammering concrete all day, your arms, shoulders, and neck feel fine after a long ride. The fork's shock absorption leaves more margin for error in your riding, which means that you might be more likely to challenge yourself with a technical climb or creek crossing.

Suspension forks are standard equipment on most mountain bikes over $600 these days, and it pays to know a little about them. The first job of a suspension system is to absorb impact to allow a bike's wheels to stay in contact with the ground, giving the rider traction and control of the bike. Its second job is to make the rider more comfortable and reduce fatigue.

The many types of suspension forks on the market change quickly with improvements in technology and the opinion of the day with regard to materials. Manufacturers use polymer rubber elastomers, metal coils, and air and oil cartridges in endless combination to achieve different rates of shock absorption and rebound. The simple, reliable design of a coil/elastomer fork provides light weight and affordability; these forks cost from $200 to $600. Fully-hydraulic oil/coil forks provide a super-plush ride and are easy to adjust and maintain, but they are heavier (3-5 pounds) and expensive ($400–$600). The newest generation of air/oil

shocks are the lightest (2-3 pounds) and cost between $400 and $600.

IMPORTANT NOTE: *Don't expect your suspension fork to work for you at first without some alterations.* Most suspension systems come out of the box set up for a 170-pound rider, so your system will likely require adjustment prior to riding. Your friendly bike mechanic should be willing and able to do this for you (of course, you'll have to pay for parts and labor). Suspension forks are set up for the weight and riding style of the rider using elastomers and springs of different weights and oils of varying viscosities. All types of suspension forks can be altered for a particular cyclist, regardless of her weight or riding style, and it is very important that your suspension be tuned correctly for you. Make sure your mechanic takes the time to get it right. You should be able to compress the fork without a lot of effort. If you feel he or she is shortchanging you, take your business elsewhere. Suspension is a useful and expensive feature, and it should work optimally.

Full Suspension: Is the Weight Worth it?

Look in any of the mountain bike magazines out there and you'll find its pages jammed with photos, articles, and ads about full suspension bikes (also referred to as "dualies," as in "dual suspension"). These bikes offer shock absorption in

While full-suspension bikes cost more and weigh more than front-suspension models, some women find the added comfort and traction well worth it.

both the front and rear. Do you need one? Reading these magazines, you might think so. But a full suspension bike is a big commitment, both because of the money you shell out ($1500–$3000) and because these bikes are heavy.

There are definite advantages to riding full suspension, however. And sometimes these advantages outweigh a few extra pounds on the frame. If you're considering a full-suspension bike, by all means, ride one first. Borrow a friend's bike or see if your bike shop has a demo in your size that you can take out on the trail for a few hours. (Riding one around the bike shop parking lot for a few minutes is probably not sufficient for you to experience either the advantages or disadvantages.) Make sure the suspension is set up correctly for your weight.

Use caution when asking male mountain bikers about full suspension. This is an area in which men and women have widely different needs. Some men are so sold on the benefits of full suspension that they don't appreciate why it might be ill-suited to some women. For a man who is 6 feet, 1 inch, 190 pounds, the advantages of full suspension are much more apparent than the disadvantages. He can lug a 30-pound full-suspension bike up a hill with much more ease than a woman who's 5 feet, 3 inches, 110 pounds. For some women, carrying around an extra three or four pounds on their bike means the difference between enjoying an all-day ride through hilly backcountry and cutting it short because they're worn out. Ask around at bike shops and among mountain bikers to find women who ride full suspension (especially women similar to you in size) and ask for their honest opinions about the advantages and disadvantages. If you can't locate a woman to ask, make sure you impress upon the males the concerns you have.

Full-suspension bikes can also be difficult to find in small sizes, making it hard for a woman 5 feet, 4 inches or under to find a bike. A few companies — VooDoo, Jamis, Marin, and Kona — have responded to the demand for smaller full-suspension bikes. Several of the bikes offered by these companies even weigh less than 26 pounds, although you pay dearly ($2,000–$3,000) for that weight savings.

If you're not mechanically minded, full suspension probably isn't the way to go. Rear suspension means more parts that can break or need adjustment. Stick with the relative simplicity of a hardtail (a bike with front, but not rear, suspension) if messing with moving parts makes you nervous.

Now for the advantages. Full-suspension bikes offer all the assets of front suspension, times two. Provided a bike is not overly heavy, full suspension allows you to climb more effectively (and stay seated longer, thus conserving energy) because your wheels track the ground better. Full suspension can reduce rider fatigue significantly. It absorbs the shock that bounces you around on a hardtail so you don't have to stand up on your pedals to let your legs absorb the shock from every bumpy section you ride through. Keep in mind that you will only appreciate the advan-

SUSPENSION SEAT POSTS: A GOOD COMPROMISE

Since many mountain bikers can't afford either the financial or weight penalties of a full-suspension bike, manufacturers offer a product that has some of the advantages of full suspension at a fraction of the price and weight. A suspension seat post absorbs small bumps, making for a more comfortable ride and allowing you to stay seated more when riding over rough terrain. Your seat post — rather than your legs — takes up some of the bumps, allowing you to conserve energy. While a suspension seat post is no substitute for true rear suspension, it can make long rides on a hardtail more comfortable. And it can be ideal for a woman who wants some of the benefits of a full-suspension bike without all the weight. Suspension seat posts cost from $60 to $200.

Sharing the wilderness: A logger gives a welcome lift to a worn-out mountain biker.

tages of a suspension system if it is tuned properly for your weight and riding style.

As prices, frame sizes, and weights shrink on full-suspension bikes, more women will find more to like about them. For a first-time mountain bike buyer, I recommend holding off on full suspension for a while. You can always trade up to full suspension later, after you better determine the kind of riding you like to do.

BIKE
ACCESSORIES

The dictionary defines an accessory as something nonessential, but useful. That's true of some, but not all, bike accessories. You won't get very far without a water bottle and cage, a spare inner tube, and an air pump, so consider these items essential. Likewise, a bike with a hard, uncomfortable saddle is unlikely to be ridden, so a comfortable saddle is essential.

SADDLES

"Does your . . . seat . . . hurt?" asks one woman of another, while squirming around on her bike's saddle.

"Front seat or back seat?" asks her friend.

"Front seat."

"No, but my back seat does."

I suspect quite a few women have heard (or had) a talk like this about bike seats. In fact, of all the reasons women give for not riding a bike, uncomfortable seats top the list. Sadly, saddles have the potential to make you sore in more than one area. If only those women knew that bike seats don't have to be a pain.

Several factors can contribute to a woman's discomfort on a bike saddle. One of the most important is simply being unaccustomed to riding a bike. If you haven't been on a bike in years, or ride infrequently, expect your rear to be a little sore until it gets used to the feel of a bike saddle again. Like getting used to a new pair of shoes, your body needs a chance to adapt to this foreign object. Don't worry. It doesn't take long. The more you ride, the stronger and firmer your butt and thigh muscles will become.

Solving Saddle Woes

While some women feel discomfort in the "back seat" or "sitting bones" area, many women experience soreness in the front as a result of pressure on the labia. Why? As we know, women are not shaped like men. Still, many women unknowingly (and uncomfortably) ride saddles designed for men. The bones that support a woman's weight when she sits down — appropriately called her "sit bones" — are a bit farther apart than a man's. What happens when a woman's sit bones extend slightly over the sides of a too-narrow saddle? All her weight rests directly on her soft genital tissues. As you might imagine, this can get painful when riding on a bumpy trail.

Many bike saddles — especially super-narrow, high-performance saddles — are too narrow for women's wider pelvises. While some women with slender hips can ride a skinny men's saddle with no discomfort, others find relief on a saddle that's slightly wider in back. Don't go too far and err on the side of a saddle that's too wide and bulky, however. A fat, squishy seat can create more problems than it solves, especially for off-road riding. The bulkiness and extra padding can chafe on long rides and detract from the feel of the bike, making effective handling harder. And a saddle that's too wide in the rear makes it hard to slide off the back — an important technique for descending.

Fortunately, most major saddle manufacturers now offer several models designed for women. The reigning queen of women's saddles is Terry Precision Cycling for Women, a woman-owned company that broke ground in the bike industry with its first women's sport saddle in 1985. I have owned a Terry women's mountain bike saddle for five years, and although the edges are worn and it has multiple tears from long-ago crashes, it's like a favorite pair of jeans — so comfortable I can't part with it.

Some women are understandably shy about discussing their saddle discomfort issues with a male bike shop employee. Not only is it embarrassing to talk about your private parts with a stranger, it can be futile, since men don't experience the same saddle problems as women. It may help to discuss your problem frankly over the phone (a little less embarrassing than face-to-face) with a knowledgeable male employee first and then go into the shop to make your purchase. Better yet, seek out a female bike salesperson, and other women who ride, for their suggestions.

Choosing a Saddle

How do you know what kind of saddle to get? Picking out a saddle should be a personal decision based on your body type and riding style. Wide or narrow, soft or firm, cutout or

CUTOUT SADDLES

Some women have found the answer to labia soreness in a cutout saddle, in which an elongated slot is cut through the nose of the saddle to alleviate pressure on the genital tissues. Sometimes the hole is obscured by the saddle's covering, and sometimes it is left open, resulting in a saddle that somewhat resembles a doughnut. A saddle with an open hole provides the added benefit of ventilation on long, hot rides, good for women who are susceptible to yeast infections or saddle sores.

Cutout saddles for men, which avoid putting pressure on the vessel that supplies blood to the penis, are also available. The Liberator line of men's and women's cutout saddles offered by Terry Precision Cycling is reportedly their fastest-selling saddle. If you have a persistent problem with genital soreness while riding, a cutout saddle is definitely worth a try.

A slight problem with labia soreness may be relieved by wearing a good pair of padded bike shorts and applying a lubricant like Vaseline or Chamois Butt'r to the short's inner liner to reduce friction. Also, make sure your saddle is level, not tilted with the nose down or up. And sometimes soreness is not due to a saddle at all, but rather an improperly fitted bike. See Chapter 8 for more tips on solving saddle soreness problems.

Water break, Canyonlands National Park, Utah. Hydration packs let you carry loads of water comfortably and conveniently.

your weight off the back when descending and allows better control of the bike in technical sections of trail and for bumpy descents. Selle San Marco, Terry, Serfas, and Giro all make high-performance mountain bike saddles for women. The guys like to ride those long, skinny, light-weight saddles for good reason — they make for more maneuverability and quicker handling on the trail. Just make sure to get one that you find comfortable. Saddles cost from $30 to $80.

WATER BOTTLES AND HYDRATION PACKS

Whether you plan to ride rugged mountain single-track or gentle rail-trails, you'll need to drink plenty of water. How much is enough? Physicians and sports medicine experts recommend drinking approximately eight ounces of water for every 30 minutes of exercise, in addition to drinking before and after the activity. Some tip-offs that you're not taking in enough water to replace what you've lost are a headache, infrequent urination, or dark-yellow urine.

not; what works wonderfully for your friend or the bike shop saleswoman might feel like a medieval torture device to you.

For starters, women who are very new to riding or who expect to ride only gentle trails for mostly short trips might consider purchasing a soft gel saddle like those made by Terry, Serfas, or Vetta to make riding more comfortable. And although it might seem illogical, a compact, lightweight saddle is best if you plan to ride more challenging trails or spend much time in the saddle, provided it fits your body. A slightly firm, narrowish saddle with a longer nose allows you to slide

How do you carry all that water on your bike? Plastic water bottles are the traditional route. Bottles usually come in 20-ounce and 28-ounce sizes. Spend the few extra dollars for quality bottles made of dense, sturdy plastic. They are less likely to leak or develop cracks. And don't forget to buy the alloy or plastic cages that hold them on the bike. Water bottles cost from $3 to $7; cages, from $6 to $13.

Most mountain bikes come with two or three sets of water bottle cage mounting bolts, usually on the down tube and/or seat tube. However, small bike frames or unusual frame designs (like "V" style or full suspension frames) can make mounting multiple water bottles a challenge. On my 14-inch Cannondale M500, the "Delta V" frame has an extremely small main triangle, making it impossible to carry more than one 20-ounce bottle (and even that's a tight fit). After discovering that 20 ounces of water is not nearly enough for a typical ride, I invested in a 90-ounce capacity CamelBak Mule and ditched the water bottle and cage altogether.

CamelBak and other manufacturers such as Blackburn and Cannondale make a fine alternative to the water bottle/cage approach — the hydration pack ($30–$80). Most of these packs consist of an inner reservoir made of polyurethane or polyethylene connected to a plastic tube with a non-leaking sip valve at the end. The reservoir is contained in a pouch designed as either a backpack or a fanny pack. I don't like the plastic taste hydration packs tend to have, but they are very convenient. They hold a large volume of water (some up to 180 ounces) and many come in handy packs that can be used to store tools, snacks, and car keys. If you're on the small side and

A hydration pack/day pack combination makes great sense for mountain bikers. Even the portable tire pump has its home.

can't imagine drinking, or carrying, 90 ounces of water on a ride, try one of the 40-ounce packs offered by CamelBak, Blackburn, and Bike Pro USA.

TIRES

At some point you may want to replace the tires that came on your mountain bike. Maybe the tread is getting worn. Or maybe you want a pair of smooth

tires with no knobs for riding on pavement.

Mountain bike tires measure 26 inches in diameter. The width you choose for your tires depends on what kind of riding you plan to do and under what conditions. Widths for mountain bike tires can vary from as narrow as 1.25 inches for a smooth tire for pavement riding to as wide as 2.2 inches for a knobby tire for super traction on trails.

Another choice is what kind of tread pattern to get. Tread patterns with many close-set knobs tend to pack up with mud and loose dirt on soft or moist ground. For riding on loose dirt or mud, a widely-spaced, knobby tread pattern allows the tire to bite into the trail surface and shed mud. For very hardpacked, dry trail surfaces, minimizing rolling resistance, rather than achieving traction, should be your concern. Tires with a shallow center tread and knobbies only on the sides allow for smooth rolling on straightaways and traction while cornering. If your mountain bike will rarely, if ever, be ridden off-road, consider using a slick tire or one with an internal-tread or grooved pattern. You'll be surprised at how much smoother and faster your ride on pavement is without the knobbies. Tires cost from $12 to $50.

Tubes and Tire Liners

Even on the shortest rides, carry a spare inner tube ($4–$8). If you get a flat on the trail, it's faster and easier

The Presta (left) is the preferred valve on high-end bikes, while the Schraeder (right) is found on most other models. Make sure your pump matches your valve.

to install a new tube than to patch a hole (but either is faster than walking your bike back to the trailhead). See Chapter 9 for illustrated, step-by-step instructions on fixing a flat. The only thing to know about tubes (besides how to change a flat one) is that they are available with one of two different valve stem designs — Presta or Schraeder. A Presta valve is a thin, long metal valve with a tiny tip that must be unscrewed before pumping air into the tube. This tip is rather delicate, so be careful not to break it off when airing up. Schraeder valves are shorter and wider, with a base made of rubber. The size of the hole in your wheel's rim dictates which style you must use. Most bikes over $700 come with rims drilled for Presta valves. Presta valves are preferred by some cyclists for their more positive seal, while other cyclists like the fact that Schraeder valves can be inflated using a gas station air hose. Before heading to the bike shop to buy a tube, you should also know what size you need. You can determine this by looking at the numbers on your tire's sidewall.

Tire liners like SpinSkins and Mr. Tuffys are plastic strips inserted between the tire and tube to guard against punctures. Off-road mountain bikers usually prefer the lighter weight SpinSkins, while many in-town cyclists swear by the thicker Mr. Tuffys for protection against glass shards and nails. Neither type of liner will prevent pinch flats, or "snakebites," which occur when your tire is underinflated and the rim impacts the inner tube as a result of a wheel slam into a pothole or rock.

PUMPS

A quality air pump is a must for mountain biking. The last thing you want is to be stranded five miles from the trailhead with no way to air up your flat tire. A small, portable pump — also called a frame pump — is usually no more than 10 inches long and can be carried in a pack or mounted to your bike's frame. Just be sure the pump is attached securely so it doesn't go flying off your bike on a bumpy downhill. Check to see that the pump converts easily from Presta to Schraeder valves so you can air up both kinds of tubes. Frame pumps cost from $15 to $50.

If you plan to do much riding, consider investing in a floor pump ($30–$50) as well. Airing up at home or at the trailhead with one of these is faster and easier than doing it on the trail with a mini pump.

TOOLS AND LUBRICANTS

Basic, routine maintenance and cleaning of your bike is necessary to keep it working properly. But even a well-maintained bike will have the occasional mechanical problem. To be prepared you should have a small assortment of tools. The following tools (in addition to an air pump and spare tube) will get you through the most common maintenance tasks and mechanical problems. For instructions on how to do basic repair and mainte-nance procedures, read Chapter 9 — Maintenance and Repair.

❶ Tire/tube patch kit (contains sev-eral patches, glue, and directions).

❷ Three tire levers.

③ Allen wrenches in 3, 4, 5, and 6 mm sizes.
④ Small adjustable wrench.
⑤ Small flat-tip screwdriver.
⑥ Chain repair tool.
⑦ Small bottle of synthetic lubricant such as Tri-Flow or Finish Line Cross Country Lube.
⑧ Frame pump.
⑨ Spare inner tube.

A multi-purpose tool ($40–$50) such as Topeak's or Blackburn's, or a mini tool kit ($13–$30) like Park's or Performance's, has many of these tools, plus several others. Other nice additions to a basic tool kit might be a rag for wiping excess lubricant from your chain and a paper towel or moist towelette to wipe grease from your hands.

GEAR TALK

BAR ENDS

Bar ends are those short, inward-curving horns of aluminum, titanium, or carbon fiber you may have seen stuck on the ends of some mountain bike handlebars. When you grip them while climbing a hill, bar ends provide leverage since they allow you to shift your weight toward the front of the bike. The fact that they allow upper body strength to be used more efficiently is especially advantageous for women.

The first time I used a pair of bar ends, I was amazed at how much easier they made climbing. They take some getting used to, though, since your hands are farther away from your shifters and brake levers (don't attempt to use bar ends on loose or rocky terrain or on technical climbs where you need your hands close to the controls).

Bar ends should be angled up 30 to 40 degrees from the handlebar; not straight up and not straight out. Be sure to cover the ends of the handlebars and bar ends with rubber or plastic end caps to protect yourself from the hard metal edges. Bar ends cost from $20 to $50.

LOCKS

Even if your style of riding consists of "load bike on car rack, drive to trail, ride, reload, and drive home," at some point, you'll probably need a bike lock ($20–$50). After hearing a few theft horror stories over the years, I recommend locking your bike whenever it is out of your sight. (For example: on the car rack in a restaurant parking lot, at the trailhead while you are using the bathroom, at the campground while you are in your tent sleeping, off the trail while you are scurrying up to a picturesque overlook for lunch, in the storage room at work, and even in the garage or basement at home.)

The strongest, most secure bike locks are the U-style locks like those offered by Kryptonite. Other companies, such as Specialized, make steel cables that are nearly as secure and more flexible. For in-town security, I suggest using two different types of locks; for example, a U-lock to secure the frame to a stationary object, and a cable to secure both wheels. This is a strong deterrent to thieves, who would need a crowbar, a pair of bolt cutters, and a lot of extra time to steal your bike. Don't forget to secure your bike's seat post and saddle (or take it with you). For security on the trail and at most campgrounds, a light cable should suffice. Most park visitors aren't likely to have packed in a pair of bolt cutters.

While U-style Kryptonite locks are the most secure, flexible steel cable locks are more versatile and allow you to secure both wheels.

RACKS

One of the advantages of a mountain bike is its ability to transport a load with minimal strain on the rider. This makes the mountain bike a perfect vehicle for commuting to work, shopping for groceries, or touring the backcountry. To do so, however, you need carrying capacity. A daypack, small backpack, or courier bag works fine for light loads. I use a Jansport book pack to carry my clean clothes, toiletries, and lunch to and from work when I ride. But for heavier loads or to get the weight off the back and shoulders, many people employ a rack ($20–$100).

♀

ESSENTIALS

"With some of my accessory purchases,
I've learned the hard way what's essential
and what's a waste of money. Early on, I
bought a suspension stem for my rigid
frame bike and initially I thought it was
great because it made my wrists and
hands more comfortable. Later, when I
bought my Stumpjumper, I was amazed
at how much a suspension fork actually
improved my riding. That flex stem was
solely a comfort feature, while the suspension fork made riding more comfortable *and* gave me more traction by
keeping the front wheel on the ground."

Angie Sheehy, salesperson,
St. Charles, Missouri

A rack should be strong and
lightweight. Bruce Gordon, Blackburn, and Rhode Gear all make
quality racks. Racks can be mounted
on the front or rear of the bike via
several small metal eyelets that are
brazed or welded on the frame. The
front and/or rear suspension on some
mountain bikes can make it difficult
to attach a rack because of the lack
of mounting eyelets. But with a little
ingenuity, you can equip a suspended
mountain bike with a rear cargo rack.
Several companies, like Topeak,
Blackburn, and Headland Bicycle
Accessories, make a rack that
attaches to the bike's seat post. These
racks aren't quite as heavy-duty as
the traditional-mount and can usually
carry no more than 15 or 20 pounds.

But they do allow you to carry a bit of
cargo when the need arises.

What can you strap to a mountain bike rack? Side-mounted bags
called panniers, top-mounted rack
bags, and child carriers are just a few
of the accessories made to attach to
racks. I've also seen briefcases,
laundry baskets, books, loaves of
bread, and milk crates carrying pup-
pies. The most interesting thing was a
chicken-wire cage containing a tow-
ering mass of aluminum cans.

BAGS

No matter what stuff you need to
carry while you ride, you can be confident that there is a bike bag for
every purpose. Bags and panniers are
manufactured by Blackburn, Cannondale, Performance, Madden Moun-
taineering, and Lone Peak.

Under-seat wedge packs
($10–$20) attach underneath your
seat to the saddle rails and seat post
and are handy for holding a spare
tube, tire levers, and keys. I use a
Blackburn mini wedge for this purpose. The larger seat packs can hold
much more. Carrying stuff in a seat
pack allows you to keep your cargo
weight close to your center of gravity
where you feel it less.

Triangle frame packs ($20–$30)
are another good way to keep weight
toward the center of the bike. These
packs fit snugly within the main triangle of your bike's frame to carry
small items like snacks, money, and

a multi-tool. However, they may not fit if you have a small or unusually shaped frame with a sloping or angled top tube, or carry a water bottle on your down tube. Frame packs can also be a nuisance if you need to carry your bike often.

Panniers (also called saddlebags) are mounted on the sides of racks. You can use a pair or one at a time. Like most bike bags, panniers ($50–$200) are usually constructed of

A fully-laden bike can carry a surprising amount of gear, as this tourer near Crested Butte, Colorado, proves.

Cordura nylon and should have strong, uniform stitching, heavy-duty zippers, and quality mounting hardware. If you plan to ride rugged trails with loaded panniers, make sure they are up to the task. The attachment device should keep the pannier

locked securely to the rack so it doesn't come flying off.

Rack-top bags ($30–$50) are favorites of commuters and casual riders for keeping food and drinks cold (some are insulated), and for carrying locks, pumps, maps, and

It dosen't look like an airliner cockpit, but a modern handlebar can sport plenty of gadgets (from top): a bell, headlight, and cyclocomputer.

baskets. They sometimes have a clear vinyl pocket on top so you can look at a map while riding. When attaching a handlebar bag, make sure the straps don't interfere with your bike's gear or brake cables.

Most performance mountain bikers prefer not to carry any extra weight over their bike's front or rear end, as it can adversely affect handling. Shying away from panniers, handle bar bags, and rack-top bags, they stick to back-packs, fanny packs, and seat

other incidentals. Take note of how the bag attaches to the rear rack before buying. They can be difficult to attach and remove.

Handlebar bags ($30–$50) are the modern equivalent of handlebar packs to carry neccessities. However, for long-distance touring, bike commuting, or day rides on gentle trails, it can be a relief to let your bike — rather than your body — bear the load.

LIGHTS AND REFLECTORS

Why would you want lights or reflectors on your mountain bike? If you use the bike for any utilitarian purpose, lights allow you to extend your trips — to the grocery store, to the movies, home from work — into the evening safely. And if you've ever taken a nighttime spin on a winding trail lit only by the moon and your bike light, you know what a thrill it can be.

The goals when riding after dark are to see and be seen. In order to be seen at night by the drivers of approaching cars as well as your riding mates, you'll need pedal reflectors ($2–$4), a flashing red rear light ($10–$20), and a white-beam headlight. Spoke reflectors, reflective tape, and/or reflective clothing also help. While reputable bike stores refuse to sell a bike not equipped with reflectors, check to make sure yours has them. If you are rarely out after dark

This bike's top tube sports a VistaLite battery pack to power a bright headlight.

and don't anticipate any all-night bike rides in the woods, a small, battery-operated low-watt light ($15–$25) like Cateye's or Specialized's should

GEAR TALK

CYCLOCOMPUTERS

Cyclocomputers are small handlebar-mounted devices that display useful information such as your current speed, average speed, distance ridden, pedal rpm's, and sometimes even altitude. They can be handy for determining how far you have yet to go on a trail or route without mile markers, or for getting the most out of your workout. Manufacturers include Avocet, Cateye, and Vetta. Cyclocomputers cost from $20 to $90.

the long run, and the amount of light they put out is astounding. Manufacturers of these systems include VistaLite, Nightsun, and NiteRider. Lighting systems usually include a 10-watt or higher headlight, a rechargeable battery, a charging adaptor, and a battery-mounting pack. Headlights can be mounted to either helmet or handlebars.

A flexible plastic fender with plenty of clearance between it and the tire is the way to go for protection from mud and water.

provide plenty of light so others can see you.

For regular night rides on- or off-road, a rechargeable high-powered lighting system is your best bet. While the initial investment is considerable ($100–$200), you'll save money and disposable batteries in

FENDERS

I will never understand why so few Americans use bike fenders, especially since there are so many lightweight, functional designs on the market today. Fenders ($12–$30) cover the wheels to prevent water, mud, or icy slush from spraying up on you. For mountain bikes used exclusively on pavement, full-wrap fenders on front

Urban accessories: A rear-view mirror (left), while it can be helpful, is no substitute for turning your head and looking back over your shoulder safely. A bell (right) can help make pedestrians and motorists take notice of you.

and back provide the most spray protection. They keep your clothes clean and dry; nice any time of year, essential in winter. These fenders have stays that bolt onto the bike. Metal fenders rattle and bend. Plastic fenders are better, and are made by Zefal. Don't use full-wrap fenders on muddy trails or roads, as mud tends to pack between tire and fender.

For a mountain bike used both on- and off-road, I suggest the front and rear partial fenders offered by Headland. These lightweight plastic protectors attach easily and quickly to your bike's downtube and seat post to keep you from getting wet. And since there's plenty of clearance between tire and fender, you don't have to worry about getting stopped in your tracks by packed-up mud.

A rear rack will also catch some of the spray thrown up by the rear wheel.

MIRRORS

On a bike used strictly for off-road riding, I find little use for a mirror. However, if you use your bike on roads as well as off, a mirror can be helpful, as it allows you to see approaching cars. Do not, however, rely on a mirror to let you know what's coming up behind you. You should still listen and look for vehicles on the road.

Mirrors ($12–$20) come in helmet-mounted, eyeglass-mounted, or handlebar-mounted styles. On my old Schwinn Crossroads commuting bike, I used a Rhode Gear handlebar-mounted mirror until it broke off when the bike fell. I haven't replaced it and can't say that I miss it much. Look for helmet- and eyeglass-mounted mirrors by CycleAware and Third Eye and handlebar-mounted mirrors by Mountain Mirrycle.

HORNS AND BELLS

Horns and bells are some of those accessories that I decide I need every time I ride in the city, but by the time I get home I've forgotten about them. The light ringing of a handlebar bell ($6–$10) is good for riding on busy park paths and in congested business districts to let slower riders, pedestrians, or dogs know you're approaching. When it comes to motorists, however, bring out the big guns. A blaring horn ($10–$20) or shrill police-style whistle ($5–$15) can pierce through the hum of traffic, through car windows and loud radios, and through a motorist's rush hour–induced stupor, making it useful for city riding. Incredibell makes a popular handlebar-mounted bell, and several companies make air or electronic horns guaranteed to grab attention.

CAR RACKS

Rooftop car racks have become a status symbol in the last decade. Even people who rarely ride a bike like the sporty and adventurous statement their rooftop rack makes about them. But for small women or those with limited upper body strength, these racks aren't all they're cracked up to be. Such women may want to forgo the lifting involved with rooftop car racks in favor of a rear-mount or hitch-style rack. Rear mounts are the least expensive ($60–$150) and very secure, as long as they are correctly mounted on the car. I have used the same Rhode Gear Super Cycle Shuttle on my Saturn for nearly four years, and with the addition of a few bungees to strap down the bikes, it's served me very well. (Tie a sock or some cloth around the pedal closest to your vehicle so as to not scratch the paint.) One disadvantage to rear-mount bike racks is they cannot be locked or permanently attached to your vehicle, making theft a possibility. Saris and Thule also make rear-mount racks.

Hitch-mounted racks are more expensive ($100–$200) and require a vehicle with a receiver hitch. These racks allow up to four bikes to be carried at once. Thule, Yakima, and Rhode Gear make receiver hitch-mounted racks.

Women who are short, but who want to use a rooftop bike rack, will appreciate Yakima's AnkleBiter mounting unit. It holds bikes by the crankarm, rather than the downtube, making it slightly less of a stretch to load and unload a bike. Other rooftop racks are made by Thule and Performance. Rooftop car racks cost from $200 to $300.

CLOTHING

By now, I'm sure you've heard that helmets are requisite safety gear for riding a bike. Some states, like Florida, have even passed legislation requiring all cyclists to wear helmets. Since nearly two-thirds of all bike accident deaths result from head injuries, don't depend on the law to make you wear a helmet. Do it for yourself. Whether you ride to work, to the park, or in the woods; whether you ride fast or slow, a helmet will protect your head in the event of a crash.

For mountain bikers who ride off-road, a helmet makes even more sense. Plenty of tumbles — even at low speed — have convinced me of that. My helmet has protected my head, face, and eyes from low-hanging branches (not to mention rocks, roots, and logs) on the trail. Some helmets are designed to absorb shock on impact by partial destruction of the outer shell and inner styrofoam, so if your helmet suffers a severe blow, replace it. It may have sustained damage you can't see.

Like bike technology, helmet technology improves every year. If you haven't tried on a helmet in the last five years, you'll be amazed at their ventilation and light weight today. And for heaven's sake, don't let vanity prevent you from wearing a helmet. The sleek, stylish ones now

A helmet protects your head only when it fits and is properly adjusted.

Cratoni makes lightweight helmets in a wide range of sizes — including very small — with excellent ventilation and cool looks. Giro and Bell also make good helmets in a variety of prices, styles, and sizes (ranging from extra-extra small to extra large). Orange Cycle's Angel Pasquale is so convinced of the superior quality of Giro and Bell products that she says other helmet manufacturers — especially bike manufacturers with their own helmet lines — are "just dabbling in it." Helmet prices range from $30 to $130. Prices are affected by a helmet's ventilation (more holes means more expensive), weight, and looks.

A helmet should sit squarely on top of your head in a level position, not tilted back. The front of the helmet should rest on the center of your forehead. To check for a cor-

on the market are a far cry from the goofy mushroom caps of the past. Look for tips on dealing with helmet hair in Chapter 7.

GEAR TALK

WHAT TO LOOK FOR IN A HELMET

- ANSI, ASTM, or Snell Foundation certification
- Snug, comfortable fit, with nothing poking you
- Self-adhesive (Velcro) foam pads to customize fit and absorb sweat
- Hard, slick outer shell that slides on impact
- Vents for cooling airflow
- Comfortable straps and fasteners
- Stabilizer/retention system to hold helmet firmly on your head
- Visor to keep sun glare and rain out of your eyes
- Good looks; a design and color you like so you'll wear it
- Ponytail-compatible design (if you have long hair)
- Lifetime crash replacement guarantee

rect, snug fit, put the helmet on but don't fasten the straps, then shake your head. The helmet shouldn't wobble around. When you're riding, your helmet should not gradually shift forward over your eyebrows, or rearward to expose your forehead. If it does, it's too big or not fitted properly. When fastened, the straps should both be taut. If the helmet can be tipped forward, tighten the back straps. If it can be tipped backward, tighten the front straps. If your straps are too long, you can cut off the excess material and use a match to carefully melt the ends so the woven nylon doesn't unravel.

CLOTHING
Natural vs. Synthetic Fabrics

Stretchy, clingy, synthetic fabrics like Lycra spandex offer complete freedom of movement and aerodynamics for cyclists. But some synthetic fabrics designed for cycling provide another important benefit: they are breathable and moisture-wicking.

Stick with helmets made by manufacturers, like Bell (top) and Giro, that specialize in them, and make sure your helmet meets ANSI and Snell safety standards.

The fibers in technical fabrics like CoolMax and MicroSelect are twisted in such a way that they draw moisture away from the skin to the outside of the fabric where it can evaporate. Natural fibers like cotton don't do that. Sure, cotton clothing can be loose and airy, but when you sweat it acts like a sponge, holding moisture against the skin and taking a long time to dry out. In hot weather, that sponge effect makes you feel moist and hot — an icky combination. In cool weather, sweaty, clinging cotton clothing can be downright dangerous, since it can make you colder when the temperature drops or when riding into the wind. That's not to say that any old synthetic fabric will perform well. Cheap polyesters can make you feel like you're wearing Saran Wrap. If a garment's hang tag or catalog description doesn't make any claims about the fabric's technical characteristics, it probably doesn't have any.

Though bike clothing can seem overly flashy and expensive, much of it serves its purpose well. Shorts like these, with a chamois-padded crotch, are a must.

Many manufacturers of cycling clothing now make shorts and tops in cotton/Lycra or cotton/CoolMax blends. This is especially prevalent in women's lines. If you love the look and feel of cotton, you may like this clothing, but don't expect it to have the same moisture-wicking capabilities of a 100 percent synthetic.

Other specialty synthetic fabrics are designed to insulate you from the cold (polyester fleece), protect you from wind and water (densely woven or laminated microfiber polyester), and reflect light at night (polyester with reflective material woven in).

One natural fiber that performs nearly as well as synthetics for cycling clothing is wool. Until the 1970s, most cycling clothing was knit from finely spun wool, which has wicking and breathability characteristics similar to those found in the best synthetics. Since wool shuns wetness and insulates, many cyclists still insist on wool jerseys, tights, socks, and arm/leg warmers for cool or wet weather riding. Another plus: Today's wool cycling clothes are machine washable. Women's wool or wool-blend jerseys are made by SporTobin and Swobo.

Now, this doesn't mean you should throw out your cotton T-shirts and go buy a drawerful of new cycling clothing. Cotton is fine for easy rides and days when the temperature and humidity are moderate. But for all-out, hard riding, and in hot, cold, or wet weather, synthetics and wool simply perform better. If you can only afford to buy one piece of cycling clothing, make it a pair of padded shorts.

Shorts and Pants

When I started mountain biking, I was decidedly low-tech when it came to clothing. My usual cycling outfit consisted of black cotton leggings (to protect myself from scratches and poison ivy), a T-shirt, a pair of old Keds, and a cotton baseball cap under my $30 helmet. Sure, I got teased by my bike shop friends who rode decked out in the latest flashy garb. But I thought all the slick, super-expensive clothes and wrap-around shades were just pretentious posing. Having a brand name emblazoned across the front of my shirt is just not me. But I have come to realize that some strange-looking cycling clothes serve their intended purpose very well and maybe aren't so silly after all. Padded shorts are one such item.

THE CHAMOIS True cycling shorts have a pad in the crotch called a chamois (pronounced "shammy") made of synthetic or cotton fabric or leather. Back in the old days, when cycling shorts were made of tightly fitting wool, all chamois were leather. Now most shorts are Lycra spandex and chamois are synthetic

---

ASK THE EXPERT

EILEEN LORSON

APPAREL/PRODUCTION MANAGER, Terry Precision Cycling for Women, Macedon, New York

Q: What problems do women typically have when shopping for bike clothing?

A: In the not so distant past, women wore men's cycling clothing because that's all there was. We wore men's jerseys that were too long and had elastic that hit us at the worst spot possible — right across the hips. We wore men's cycling shorts with a too-large waist and too-narrow hips that were usually too long in the legs.

Now, thankfully, more companies are making cycling clothing for women. Manufacturers finally realized that women are not interested in looking like boys on the road and trail. We want clothes that fit, perform, and are flattering, comfortable, and easy to care for. The biggest problem women have now is that their local bike shop may not stock much women's clothing, or doesn't stock it in a wide range of sizes. Another problem is that many clothing manufacturers don't make a wide range of sizes for women. Women don't just come in small, medium, and large.

shorts will have a synthetic, moisture-wicking, perforated chamois to keep you dry and comfortable. The chamois should have a woman-specific cut, somewhat like an hourglass, so there isn't extra material bunching up between your legs. It should be thick enough to provide a cushion to sit on and long enough to cover you in the front as well as the back. A woman's chamois usually has two parallel seams running down

Riding for any length of time without padded cycling shorts is a guarantee that something painful will happen to your rear end. These Lycra spandex shorts are also very aerodynamic.

fabric. A chamois' primary function is to give you a layer of protection to prevent skin chafing. It also cushions your sit bones and sensitive genital tissues.

A good pair of women's bike

the center of the pad which attach it to the short. Chamois with just one center seam (found in men's bike shorts) can irritate women's genitals.

Bike shorts are designed to be worn without underpants, and

wearing them defeats the purpose of wearing bike shorts. Underpants have seams at the crotch and leg openings that can rub and chafe. Also, underpants are usually made of cotton, which holds moisture, or nylon, which doesn't breathe. Both those properties create a perfect environment for a yeast infection.

Some women (and manufacturers) claim that a chamois containing an anti-bacterial agent is important for preventing problems like saddle sores and yeast infections. But I'm not convinced it's necessary or prudent to use an anti-bacterial chamois. I prefer not to put my privates in constant contact with chemicals. Starting out with a clean, dry chamois and changing out of sweaty shorts as soon as possible after a ride usually lets you avoid yeast infections. Women who are in the saddle for long periods of time

THE "UNISEX" DEBATE

Sometimes, when a bike shop runs out of women's bike shorts, the sales staff will try to encourage women customers to buy the "unisex" shorts on the rack. But many women cyclists, including Eileen Lorson of Terry Precision Cycling, disagree with the idea of unisex bike shorts.

"No clothing is unisex. Men and women do not have unisex bodies. As Georgena Terry (founder and CEO of Terry Precision Cycling for Women) says, 'Unisex clothing means we wear men's clothing.' Does a unisex jersey have darts or extra fabric to accommodate a woman's bust? Do unisex shorts have a narrower waist or larger hips to fit a woman's body? Of course not. Things are changing, but it's still a man's world."

Angel Pasquale, a clothing and accessories buyer for Orange Cycle in Orlando, Florida, calls the idea of unisex bike shorts "hogwash."

"That's just so bike shops don't have to buy women's shorts. Women's shorts simply fit women better. They are cut specifically for women, with curves in the places women have curves. Unisex shorts also typically have a center seam, which can irritate women's genitals."

That said, there are a few women who actually fare better with unisex or men's shorts than with women's. Women who are tall or who are built more straight than curvy, with slender thighs and slim hips, can sometimes wear men's or unisex shorts successfully, provided the chamois works for them.

and prone to saddle sores find that applying a lubricant like Body Glide or Chamois Butt'r to the chamois keeps it soft to reduce friction. See Chapter 8 for more tips on preventing and treating saddle sores and yeast infections.

WHAT ELSE TO LOOK FOR IN SHORTS
Look for a women's short, which will be cut to accommodate a woman's shape — fuller in the hips and thighs, slimmer in the waist. The waistband should not be so tight that it cuts into your waist when you bend over your handlebars. For a more form-fitting fit, look for six- or eight-panel shorts, rather than four-panel. More expensive shorts have more panels for a better fit.

Many companies now make women's shorts in a shorter length than is traditional for cycling shorts, with a 5-inch, rather than an 8-inch inseam. Some women like the look of this shorter length, along with the higher tan line that results. I like them because I'm short, and regular-length bike shorts are frequently too long for me. One risk you run with these shorter shorts — especially if you are tall — is subjecting your bare thighs to chafing on the sides of your saddle.

Another option for easy mountain biking and around-town riding is double shorts that have a padded chamois liner underneath a cotton or Supplex baggy short. I use this type of short for commuting to work and running errands on my bike because they are less conspicuous than a pair of skintight bike shorts. The casual observer can't tell that they're bike shorts at all and they come in a beautiful variety of colors — pale lime green, deep sea green, and vivid grape, to name a few. I don't recommend these shorts for challenging off-road rides, as the outer short can restrict movement and get caught on your saddle.

Some companies that make excellent bike shorts for women include Pearl Izumi, Andiamo, Terry, Shebeest, and Bellwether. Cycling shorts range in price from $30 to $80.

ASK THE EXPERT
KAREN JOHNSON
SPORT CLASS RACER,
St. Louis, Missouri

"I'm tall, slim, and not very busty, and most women's bike clothing is made for smaller women. I skip the women's tops and go with men's because they fit better. I find that I like men's jerseys better anyway. The fabrics are thinner and cooler, they have longer zippers for ventilation, and there are none of those annoying darts."

TIGHTS When I was a beginning mountain biker, I had a terrible time with poison ivy, which is rampant in the Missouri Ozarks where I ride. No matter how hard I tried to avoid it, two to three days after a great ride the itchy, oozing blisters would reveal themselves and plague me for days. My solution was drastic, but well worth it — tights. For several years, I wouldn't set foot in the woods without ankle-to-hip coverage. Even in hot Mid-

Tights provide protection from poison ivy and from the cold, rain, and wind. Most don't have padded crotches; wear them over padded cycling shorts.

western summers, I was obsessive about keeping my legs covered. Luckily, I'm not quite as susceptible to poison ivy as I once was and I wear shorts on most summer rides now. But I'm still a believer in tights for the times when you want leg pro-

tection or insulation from cold, rain, or wind.

Most tights don't have a chamois, so they should be worn over shorts that contain one. Women's tights ($40–$80) are made by Bellwether and Pearl Izumi.

A sports bra/top, while not a necessity, is surprisingly comfortable compared to a T-shirt.

Tops

A cycling shirt is probably not one of those things you're going to buy in the beginning. I didn't. I wore cotton T-shirts, tank tops, sports-bra tops, even a bikini top when I started riding. Keep in mind, though, that cotton gets droopy and clingy when it's wet. When you're sweaty and your neckline and armholes are sagging, that's when you're guaranteed to meet up with the best-looking guy on the trail.

While a cycling-specific shirt is not essential, it sure is nice. After you've been riding for a while, try one and you'll be pleasantly surprised at how much more comfortable it is than a T-shirt. Cycling shirts come in many

CLOTHING FOR LARGER WOMEN

Finding women's bike clothes in large sizes can be difficult. Angel Pasquale says it's her biggest complaint with clothing manufacturers.

"Companies are finally making innovative, appealing clothing for women, but they don't have their sizing on target. In many cases, the larges are medium, the mediums are small, and the smalls are teeny-tiny. For larger women, quality clothing is hard to find. Sure, they can wear a men's large, but they get into the same old problems: crotch seams, no women's cuts, no bust, no hips," says Pasquale.

Sugoi, she says, offers a good selection of large sizes, and their cut seems more generous than other manufacturers'. Mt. Borah Designs makes a baggy cycling short, an 8-panel Lycra/cotton short, and a cycling liner brief for women in L, XL, and XXL. Extra large size clothing by Dirt Designs, SporTobin, Terry, and Pearl Izumi may also fit some larger women.

different styles, fabrics, and colors, and I'm happy to report that many of them fit women beautifully. There are hip-looking wool jerseys, airy fitted tank tops, and elegant tops that can make the transition from trail to town. If you like clothes shopping, you'll have a blast looking at all the women's cycling tops on the market.

A cycling shirt should fit close to your skin to allow the fabric to function optimally, wicking sweat and providing a sleek profile. For the best moisture transfer, get 100 percent synthetic. If you don't like the clingy, racer look, many of the looser-fitting, cotton-look women's tops on the market perform adequately. Just remember, the less cotton, the better if you want to avoid wet clothes.

Look for necklines that won't reveal more than you're comfortable with when you bend over your handlebars. Ditto for armholes. Some

---

GEAR TALK

BENEFITS OF A CYCLING JERSEY

VENTILATION/MOISTURE WICKING Close-fitting, synthetic or wool cycling jerseys pull sweat away from your skin to the outside of the fabric, where it can evaporate to keep you dry and comfortable.

FREEDOM OF MOTION Stretchy knit jerseys allow you to move more freely than some other fabrics, like woven cotton.

AERODYNAMICS Smooth, close-fitting clothing offers a slight advantage over loose, billowy garments in minimizing drag. Perhaps more importantly for mountain biking, it also prevents you from getting hung up on tree branches or your saddle.

VISIBILITY This feature is essential if you ride your mountain bike on the road to commute to work, run errands, or get to a trailhead. It's also a good way to alert hunters and other trail users to your presence. They'll notice you sooner if you wear a Day-Glo orange jersey, rather than an earth-toned T-shirt.

There are other, more subjective benefits of wearing a cycling jersey, not the least of which is that they look cool. I think the supple form of a strong cyclist sprinting down the trail in sleek clothing is attractive (although some people still insist it just looks weird). Then there's the hammer factor. I feel like a pro when I'm wearing a jersey, like a casual amateur when I wear a T-shirt. When I want to really push myself, I wear the jersey. When I want to take it easy, I wear the T-shirt.

This cycling top provides both cooling ventilation and a feminine style statement.

cropped style. If you'll be riding a trail that's overgrown in places, it's nice to have the protection of sleeves. For rugged trail riding, look for clothing designed for mountain biking, as it is usually more durable than road bikewear. For hot-weather trail riding, I like to wear a synthetic sports bra/top that dries quickly so I can cool off in any lakes or streams I might pass. Hot-weather riding necessitates thin, cooling fabrics and long front zippers for ventilation. Many jerseys have handy back pockets for carrying a snack, but unless they're zippered, don't pocket anything you can't afford to lose. If you wear a hydration or fanny pack, pockets are unnecessary.

Numerous companies — including all the clothing manufacturers previously mentioned — make cycling tops for women.

women prefer the coverage of a waist-length tank top, rather than a

---

ASK THE EXPERT

VALERIE SALAZAR

SALESPERSON, Mesa Cycling, St. Louis, Missouri

Q: What advice do you have for women who are looking for bike clothing?

A: Look around to find female-specific options. It's worth the search for better fit and styling. And once you find something you really like, don't be afraid to spend the money on quality clothes. Also, if you're a serious cyclist, don't shy away from a close fit. Many of my female customers who have been cycling for years are surprised when they try on a women's jersey for the first time. They always ask, "Is this too tight?" They're so used to wearing men's jerseys that fit loosely and leave a bundle of fabric around the waist.

Shoes

A pair of old gym or hiking shoes will suffice for new mountain bikers, as long as the shoes are not too wide to fit in your toe clips. Tie the laces tightly and tuck the loops inside the shoe so they don't get hooked on your chain rings. If you find that you're riding often and want better performance, you can find it in a cycling shoe.

What makes a shoe a cycling shoe? A rigid sole is the most important quality. A stiff sole transfers power to the pedal better than a flexible one and prevents the bottom of your foot from becoming sore from constant pressure on the pedal. If you ride mostly paved or gentle trails or gravel roads, Cannondale and Specialized make casual cycling shoes that look and act much like hiking boots, but with stiffer soles. For more rugged trail riding, bike shoes should have aggressive tread on the bottoms for the times when you need to dismount and walk through a tricky section. They should also be fairly lightweight, as heavy shoes weigh you

Touring shoes for mountain biking are easy to walk in while still featuring a rigid sole. The extra contour in the soles of more expensive shoes helps in transferring energy to the pedals efficiently. High-performance mountain biking shoes feature greater sole rigidity and contour, with cleats for clipless pedal systems recessed in the sole to facilitate walking.

down. If you use toe clips, make sure your bike shoe is easy to get in and out of the clip. I prefer shoes that fasten with Velcro straps, rather than laces, because there's no risk of the laces becoming untied or getting caught on the chain rings. If you ride mostly in warm weather, get a shoe with plenty of breathable mesh. The mesh lets air in to cool your foot and lets water out after you've ridden through a stream. Removable insoles are a good feature because you can pull them out after riding to let your shoes dry faster. In cool weather, remove them to provide more room for thick socks.

For the woman who likes long rides and/or rugged trails, I strongly suggest upgrading to clipless pedals. The improved performance is worth the extra expense and the time necessary to learn to use them. Most mountain bike shoes on the market are compatible with clipless pedals.

They should have a recess for the pedal cleat on the outer sole.

Unfortunately, shoes are one area where women still have limited choices. There are few woman-specific shoes on the market, and most bike shoes are cut a little wide for women, who tend to have narrower feet than men. Mail-order companies like Performance offer small sizes primarily in lower-priced shoe models, and many bike shops don't stock shoes in sizes smaller than women's size 9! (This can be a big disappointment when you're planning an epic ride for the next day and need shoes NOW.) Plan ahead and order shoes in your size.

Luckily, there are a few very good shoes out there that work well for women. Shimano has an excellent line of shoes in various price ranges that come in small sizes and perform well. Diadora's Chiliwoman mountain bike shoe gets raves from mountain bike racers. Sidi's Toscana shoe is pricey, but fits women very well. And Lake's women's mountain bike shoe is another good choice. Bike shoes cost from $40 to $130.

Jackets

A waterproof jacket stuffed into your bike bag weighs next to nothing and can keep you from getting chilled in an unexpected rain shower. Look for breathable fabrics like GoreTex or Ultrex, or vents under the arms and along the back to let body heat and condensation escape. Otherwise, you'll end up as wet on the inside of your jacket as on the outside. You'll also appreciate a jacket with a fairly close fit that doesn't billow out when you pick up speed. If your rain jacket isn't waterproof, you can use one of

■

ASK THE EXPERT
ANGEL PASQUALE
CLOTHING AND ACCESSORIES
BUYER, Orange Cycles,
Orlando, Florida

Q: How have things changed over the years for women when it comes to finding cycling clothing?
A: It's much, much easier now to find women's cycling clothing than it was ten or even five years ago. I think the main reason is that women have broken into the industry to become designers and clothing reps. These industry women are responsible for the interesting fabrics, designs, and better fits that we see today. Cannondale, for instance, has a woman in charge of their clothing line and it's helped a lot. Also, there are more women involved in cycling, so the demand is higher. We kept asking and asking for clothing, and manufacturers and stores finally got the message.

the wash-in waterproofing treatments sold by Nikwax and others. While they're not a permanent solution (they must be reapplied after several washings), they're inexpensive and have kept me dry on trips through Washington's Olympic Peninsula rain forests. You're better off getting a jacket in a highly visible color like yellow or orange for those rainy or dusky times when you might have to ride on the road. Pearl Izumi and Bellwether make quality jackets in women's cuts and sizes. Jackets range from $50 to $120.

Look for a lightweight, fairly close-fitting waterproof jacket that can be easily stuffed into your bike bag, ready to be donned when rain or chill call for it.

Miscellaneous

GLOVES Gloves ($15–$50) prevent sore hands and blisters, give a better grip on the handlebars, protect your hands when you fall, and absorb vibration from the trail or road. I consider gloves essential riding gear. For warm weather riding, fingerless gloves are fine. But in cooler weather, full-fingered gloves offer not only warmth, but an extra measure of protection. Choose a snug, comfortable glove with a well padded palm and an absorbent

Fingerless cycling gloves prevent blisters and provide better grip on the handlebars.

bras for cycling are stretchy sports bras ($20–$40) made of CoolMax or ones with a CoolMax liner and Supplex or Lycra on the outside. This allows sweat to wick through the fabric and evaporate. Depending upon your build, if you are riding rough trails you may need a fairly supportive bra, like a JogBra. It's also nice to find a crop top that doubles as a sports bra so you can wear it by itself on hot days.

ARM AND LEG WARMERS Ingenious little inventions, leg and arm warmers ($20–$40) are a great alternative to wearing full tights or a long-sleeved jersey when the weather's cool. Made of the same synthetic materials as jerseys and shorts, they slip on and off quickly and take up very little space in your bike bag. You don't even have to take off your shoes to remove them if it warms up mid-ride. I prefer leg warmers to waterproof, nylon rain pants on cold, wet rides, since the stretchy fabric dries quickly and allows me more freedom of motion.

If you're slender, be sure to get arm and leg warmers that won't slide down your limbs as you ride. Shebeest, Koulius Zaard, and Pearl Izumi make warmers in sizes to fit small or slender women.

KNEE AND ELBOW PADS Some mountain bikers wear padding to protect vulnerable areas, especially when riding challenging single-track trails. Cross-country mountain bike racer Michele Keane wore elbow

patch of terry-cloth on the thumb to wipe sweat or a sniffly nose (a good reason to make sure they are machine washable).

Pearl Izumi, Grandoe, Terry, and Cannondale all make gloves sized for a woman's smaller hands. However, finding full-fingered winter gloves that fit can be a challenge. I still haven't found a pair of cold weather gloves that fit and keep my hands sufficiently warm.

BRAS I find regular bras uncomfortable for active riding, as the straps and fasteners chafe, pinch, and bind. Besides, they're usually made of nylon (hot, non-breathable) or cotton (holds moisture). The best

pads and Tioga kneepad knickers for a year and a half to build her confidence while downhilling, until the knickers' crotch seams (they were men's pants) began to bother her. Other protective padding brands include Crash Pads and Sugoi's Body Armor arm and leg warmers.

SUNGLASSES

Since I'm nearsighted and have never solved the wind and dust issues of wearing contact lenses on the trail, I wear my prescription glasses. The trails I ride are usually shaded enough that glare is not a problem, and my glasses protect my eyes from flying bugs and tree branches. As a result, I've never gotten into the habit of wearing sunglasses on the

A synthetic fleece-lined jacket is comfortable and warm, sheds moisture well, and is much lighter than wool — something to think about if you're packing for a long ride.

trail. However, they are essential when I'm on the road to protect my eyes from glare.

Get sunglasses with interchangeable lenses (dark, medium,

Shades can be functional, as well as look cool, by protecting your eyes from debris and tree branches and by preventing tearing.

While far from sleek and stylish, a waterproof poncho can be the best way to stay the course through foul weather.

and clear) that can be worn in a variety of light conditions. Be sure to choose lenses that filter out UVA rays. Wrap lenses and frames protect your eyes from dust, pollen, and wind, which cause the eyes to water. Watery eyes can make for a dangerous ride if you're blinking back tears when you should be concentrating on the trail. Smith, Zeal, and Performance make sunglasses with a low profile, a narrow frame, and short temples that fit small faces better.

LEARNING
TO
RIDE
OFF-ROAD

In 1985, Adrienne Murphy bought her first mountain bike. A competitive road cyclist, runner, and triathlete, she liked the freedom of traveling through the woods on a bike. But the small group of people who rode mountain bikes in her hometown at the time were all men.

"I learned from the guys. I'm very athletic and driven, so I stuck with it. But it was frustrating since they were already proficient and pretty fast. Since I was always at the back of the pack, I pretty much taught myself how to ride. It took a long time."

As Adrienne rose through the ranks of local, regional, and national mountain bike racing, eventually turning pro, she never forgot her rough start in the sport. If other women were to enjoy mountain biking and stick with it, she decided, they would need a more appealing introduction than she'd had. As a result, she began offering mountain bike classes for women.

"I was meeting so many women who owned mountain bikes but didn't even know how to shift gears properly that I knew there was a real need for the class," Adrienne says. "I wanted women to know that mountain biking is fun and doesn't have to be intimidating."

ACHES AND PAINS

"If you're a beginner, you might have a sore neck or butt for your first ride or two, but stick with it. It doesn't take long to go away."

Isabel Dickson, mountain bike instructor, Bryson City, North Carolina

RESOURCES

If you're learning to mountain bike, there's no reason to feel like you have to do it alone. There are a number of resources to help you learn. Videos, books, and magazines provide step-by-step instructions and tips on mountain biking technique. But nothing beats hands-on learning from an experienced mountain biker, whether it's a friend or a hired instructor.

When Karen Johnson, a sport-class racer in St. Louis, Missouri, decided she wanted to be a better mountain biker so she could win some races in the local series, she went straight to the bike shop where she'd bought her bike, talked to salesman Jeremy Fields (an expert-level racer himself), and hired him as her coach.

"When I learn something, I want to learn the right way. Jeremy had the skills, the knowledge, and the attitude to help me become a stronger mountain biker."

Isabel Dickson, a mountain bike instructor at Nantahala Outdoor Center in Bryson City, North Car-

olina, highly recommends women-only mountain bike instruction classes. "Women really flourish in these classes. In a mixed-gender class, some women feel nervous about challenging themselves. They don't want to appear inept, hurt themselves, or fall behind. But since a women-only class offers a supportive environment, the vibes change; women gain confidence and try new things because they're comfortable."

See "Sources & Resources" for information about women-only skills camps.

THE IMPORTANCE OF ATTITUDE

In our air-conditioned, fast-food, take-the-elevator-not-the-stairs society, we become accustomed to a pretty cushy existence. Dealing with the bugs, heat, humidity, and hard physical exertion mountain biking can dish out is foreign to most of us.

There's no doubt that learning to mountain bike is hard work. Developing the ability to persevere and even enjoy an experience despite minor discomfort is important to becoming a successful mountain biker (and, I believe, a better person). When you can rise above what you find annoying or uncomfortable, you learn more and have more fun. Improving backcountry skills — map reading, first aid, hazard identification — makes a positive attitude easier. If you're worried about getting lost or wiping out at every turn, it's hard to relax and have a good time.

It also helps to remind yourself occasionally why you're on the trail. If I find myself getting frustrated and worried about keeping up, I stop, take some deep breaths, and appreciate how beautiful my surroundings are. Then I get back on the bike and repeat to myself, "Enjoy the ride, enjoy the ride." It works wonders.

Mountain biking can be challenging, but it shouldn't be torturous. Don't sabotage your progress and fun by riding with impatient or insensitive jerks who constantly leave you in the dust. Bring your grievances to their attention. If their attitudes don't improve, find someone else to ride with.

GETTING READY TO RIDE SINGLE-TRACK

What is single-track? For me, it's what mountain biking is all about and what mountain bikes were made for. Single-track is a narrow trail interspersed with roots, rocks, stumps, logs, and other obstacles for you to ride over, around, and through. If you're just learning to ride a mountain bike, put off your first single-track adventure until you feel very comfortable with your bike. Ride it to work, to the park, and on some gravel roads first. Ride it around a flat, grassy field. Once you feel comfort-

able, take it for a few rides on an easy, fairly level off-road trail. Work up to single-track. Some riders never take their bikes on single-track, preferring to ride paved and gravel roads and rail-trails.

If you plan to ride single-track, you need a bike that's appropriate for it. In my opinion, that doesn't mean you require suspension, front or rear. I first learned to ride the Ozarks' rocky backcountry trails on a rigid frame bike. Suspension can come later.

What you must have is correct body positioning on your bike. To put it another way, you can't ride single-track sitting up straight. Sitting in an upright position on your bike, rather than leaning over your handlebars, gives you inadequate control over the movement of your front wheel, making tight turns, hill climbs, and obstacles needlessly difficult. The ideal bike position for single-track

Riding single-track requires a level of concentration and new riding skills that, at first, will remind you of your first time on a bike.

your feet on the pedals. A stem (the part of the bike that connects handlebars to frame) that angles upward puts you in an upright position and throws your body weight onto your tailbone. This makes for too much weight over your rear wheel and a sore butt, especially on a rough trail. Many times, women mountain bikers who suffer from a sore rear end don't need distributes your weight equally among the three body/bike contact points — your butt on the saddle, your hands on the handlebars, and

TECHNIQUE TIP

RIDING SINGLE-TRACK

● Look ahead. Don't stare at obstacles you want to avoid or fixate on your front wheel. Try to keep your gaze primarily on the trail ahead about 10 to 15 feet, scanning regularly back and forth from there to just in front of your front tire.

● Choose your route. Also referred to as "picking your line," this means quickly assessing your options for traversing the trail ahead, making a decision, and sticking to it. Usually, the route chosen is the smoothest with the least obstacles. On technical trails, choosing your route is a constant process requiring almost as much mental as physical agility from the rider.

● Use speed and momentum to your advantage. Slowing to a crawl through a technical section won't get you very far. Instead, pick up your pace a bit and use the power of momentum to get you through.

a softer saddle — just a different riding position.

Unfortunately, most entry level bikes ($300–$600) put their riders in this awkward upright position. If that describes your bike, do what I did and buy a stem with a lesser angle. For single-track, your stem should angle no more than 10 degrees upward. This angle is referred to as "rise." A stem with less rise gives you quicker steering for negotiating tight turns and better leverage for lifting your front wheel over obstacles.

SHIFTING GEARS

If you've ever ridden a one-speed beach cruiser or coaster-brake bike, you'll probably remember what a

BEGINNER'S FRUSTRATION

"On one of my first mountain bike rides, I got so mad and frustrated that I threw my helmet across the trail. What broke the tension and got both me and my husband-to-be laughing was that it landed in a big pile of horse poop."

Stephanie Ashley, art teacher
Hillsboro, Missouri

drag hills were. Even the slightest grade had you huffing and puffing and pushing on the pedals with all your might to make it up. Anything more than a small hill had you off the bike and walking.

Mountain bikes — with their multiple low gears — are designed to

● Don't get mad, get even. Instead of letting a tough section psyche me out, I use several techniques to get more assertive and power through it. Sometimes it's a loud grunt. Other times, it's an authoritative order shouted at my bike.

● Don't crowd the rider in front of you. It will probably make her nervous and more likely to fall in your path.

● Try new things, but don't overdo it. Michele Keane uses what she calls the Three Times Rule: "I give myself three times to ride something. If I can't do it in three, I leave it alone and return to try it on a different day. I don't believe in beating yourself up."

● There's no shame in walking or shouldering your bike through a section you find too difficult. Just don't do it to the exclusion of trying challenging things. If your arms tire quickly when carrying your bike, try some of the upper-body strengthening exercises suggested in Chapter 5.

with each click of the left shifter. When the chain is on the smallest chain ring in the front, pedaling should be very easy. You'll use this low gear, called the "granny ring," for climbing steep hills or riding challenging terrain. Click your left shifter until the chain hops up to the middle chain

Ideal single-track body position: some weight over the handlebars and overall weight distributed evenly between the bars, the saddle, and the pedals.

ride up hills that some people might have trouble walking up. The gears are divided between three chain rings in the front and seven, eight, or nine cogs in the back. The shifters on the handlebars connect to the front and rear derailleurs via cables, allowing you to change gears. The left shifter controls the front derailleur and the right shifter controls the rear.

To practice shifting gears, go to a flat, open field, or empty parking lot. Start pedaling and then twist or click your left shifter once. *Always shift while you're pedaling.* Notice whether the shift made pedaling easier or harder. Now watch your front chain rings to see where the chain ends up

ring in the front. This gear is good for pedaling moderate off-road trails or climbing hills on pavement. Click your left shifter until your chain is on the largest chain ring in the front. Notice the increased resistance when pedaling. This higher gear propels you farther with each pedal stroke and is appropriate for riding flat off-road trails or pavement.

Next try using your right shifter. This shifter allows for gear changes in smaller increments. Go through every gear on your bike, using both shifters. With practice, you'll soon have a good idea how all the gear combinations feel and what they look like on the sprockets.

The goal of shifting gears is to

achieve a steady, easy spin, or cadence, no matter what the terrain, to allow you to maintain your pace and conserve energy. The key to shifting successfully is anticipation. When you see that you're approaching a hill or an obstacle, shift to an easier (lower) gear before you get there. If you wait until you're on the steeper grade, bearing down hard on the pedals, your shift will be accompanied by loud grinding and popping noises. This can be very disconcerting, and it's bad for your drivetrain and an inefficient use of your energy.

Many beginners shift gears very reluctantly, if at all. Get over it. Shift, shift, shift until you're comfortable and it's second nature. Pretty soon you'll be shifting smoothly and riding faster and more efficiently as a result.

■ ───────────────────────

BIKE PREP 101: A PRE-RIDE CHECKLIST

Before hitting the road, a quick check to be sure your bike is in good working order can go a long way toward assuring a safe, hassle-free ride. For further details on basic maintenance and repair procedures mentioned here, refer to Chapter 9.

❶ Check tires. Look for cuts or loose materials (for example, glass slivers) on the tread. This is especially important for mountain bikers. Stones, glass, and other sharp objects can easily get wedged into those deep treads.

❷ Inflate tires. Bike tires are inflated at much higher pressures than car tires, typically between 50 and 100 pounds per square inch (psi). Mountain bikers, seeking extra traction and more shock absorption for loose sur-faces, may start with tire pressure of 40 psi or even less. Higher pressure in a smaller tire is harder to maintain; in other words, bike tires lose air pressure much more quickly than car tires. Experienced riders often reinflate their tires before every ride.

❸ Check wheels. Make sure the wheels are tightly fastened to the frame and are properly aligned. Give both the front and rear wheels a good tug and shaking to make sure they are secure. If there is any looseness, release the quick-release flange. (All but the least expensive bikes are equipped with quick-release devices to attach wheels to frames. See Chapter 9 for details on how to adjust the quick-release device.) Give it a quick, tightening twist (or two), then resecure the

continued on page 80

continued from page 79

wheel. Make sure the wheels are aligned straight between the frame stays and the brake pads.

◐ Check brakes. Make sure the brakes are centered and the pads aligned over the rims, not the tires. Make sure cable tension is set right for accurate braking and that there is no slack in the cable.

◑ Clean and lube the chain. Quickly run a cloth with a degreasing solvent over the chain, then apply, sparingly, a thin layer of lubricant. This is not essential before every ride, but keeping your chain clean will ensure a smooth-working drivetrain.

◐ Bring water and food. Water or other fluids are essential for any ride of half an hour or more, especially in warm weather. Dehydration, announcing itself in the form of dizziness, headaches, muscle weakness, and cramps, can be not only debilitating but downright dangerous. It's better to take too much water than too little, because water you don't drink can always be used to squirt over your head or legs as a coolant. For any ride of two hours or more, you'll need easy-to-eat food (fruit, energy bars, or the like) to replenish your body's fuel supply.

◑ Bring repair gear. An extra inner tube (or tire), a pump (or compressed-air cartridges), tire irons, and a patch kit are most important. A small adjustable wrench and a set of hex (or Allen) wrenches are useful for making brake, derailleur, and seat adjustments. A screwdriver may come in handy.

◐ Look for anything obviously wrong. Loose screw, dangling cable, broken spoke, a crack in the frame—if it's broken and reparable, fix it. If you don't have the tools or the know-how, get your bike to a shop for immediate service—just don't *ride* it!

BRAKING

Getting used to your brakes early on will help you immensely on the trail. Ride around your neighborhood or a park to discover how hard you must squeeze the brake levers to stop, turn a corner, and descend a small hill. The left brake lever controls the front brake and the right lever controls the rear. Try using different amounts of pressure on each brake lever to see how the bike handles differently.

A technique called "feathering the brakes" — squeezing both brake levers lightly and intermittently to modulate speed — is indispensable in mountain biking, particularly if your bike has powerful direct-pull brakes ("V-brakes") or disc brakes. You'll know what I mean if you've ever squeezed one brake lever hard. Locking up your front brake can cause you to sail over the handlebars in an "endo." Prevent an endo by using slightly more pressure on the rear brake lever than the front. Locking up the rear brake can cause your rear wheel to skid out, making the bike feel squirrelly on gravel and other loose surfaces. Try to get comfortable with this feeling by practicing both riding out and controlling rear wheel skids. It will happen to you from time to time on loose or rocky downhill and it's good to know how to handle it.

Just as in shifting, anticipation is important in braking. Don't wait until you're in the middle of a tough section of trail to brake, or you'll lose control. Brake before you get there. However, don't brake too much or you may not have enough momentum to get through. Slow down as you approach a difficult section, choose your route, then accelerate through.

Braking while riding fast takes practice and something called Body English. Say you're riding along at a pretty fast clip on level, hardpacked ground and suddenly you see a big log across the trail. If you stay seated in your saddle and jam on the brakes you'll quite possibly endo. Instead, lift your butt off the saddle and shift your weight towards the

Be ready to brake at all times, shift your weight back, and be alert to the terrain ahead of you — key elements to riding safely on off-road terrain.

back behind the saddle, standing on the pedals. Then brake. Shifting your weight to the back in this way keeps both your wheels on the ground and you on the bike. Although I learned this technique while mountain biking, I commonly use it when I need to make a quick stop on pavement.

CORNERING

When steering a bike, very little is actually accomplished through twisting the handlebars. Most turns are primarily leans. Practice leaning into gradual turns. Anticipate turns

stroke (up), and your outside foot is at the bottom (down) to keep your weight balanced and to prevent your inside foot from banging into an obstacle.

Most riders favor one side of the body over the other when cornering. For example, I find right turns much easier than left (I'm also right-handed). If you favor one type of turn, practice making the other kind until it feels natural. Practice making wide turns, tight turns,

Good cornering form: outer leg extended, leaning in, inside knee turned out for extra balance, upper body driving aggressively through the turn.

and brake before you get to them, then accelerate through. Sharp, hairpin turns require a turn of the handlebars. They also call for a special technique in which your inside foot is at the top of the pedal and turns with obstacles. I like to do this in the trailhead parking lot, campground, or an open field while I'm waiting for my riding partners to suit up before a ride.

CLIMBING

Even if you're a beginner, start trying to tackle some small hills immediately. Climbing hills builds fitness faster than anything else. Think of it as a way to eat more chocolate. Besides, the sooner you get the hang of climbing, the sooner you can go anywhere you want on your bike.

This is where all your shifting practice comes in. When you see that big hill ahead, shift into a low gear, stay seated, and keep pedaling. Staying in the saddle to pedal in an easy gear conserves energy and helps you maintain traction. When you feel the urge to stand while climbing to maintain momentum, try shifting to an easier gear and staying seated a while longer. When you finally must stand, keep your torso forward to weight the front end of the bike and prevent it from coming off the ground. Experiment with seated and standing climbing and try using your bar ends if you have them, unless you're on a loose, rocky surface.

Don't try to impress your friends by racing up hills, especially at first. That's a good way to wear yourself

GEAR TALK

SADDLE HEIGHT

Have you ever noticed the height to which some skilled mountain bikers keep their seat posts extended? To the uninitiated, it might look unreasonably high. In fact, you might be amazed the rider doesn't pitch forward over the handlebars while she's riding.

An experienced cross-country mountain biker usually likes an aggressive posture on her bike that keeps her hands level with or slightly lower than her seat. When you're first learning to mountain bike, you'll probably feel most comfortable keeping your seat fairly low. That's fine. Just make sure that as your skills improve, you gradually raise your seat to give you more control over the handlebars and a nearly full leg extension. This position takes some getting used to, but it will greatly improve your bike's handling and pedal stroke efficiency. It can also prevent you from overstressing your knees with an insufficient saddle height.

If you're like me, you'll change your saddle height frequently when you're learning to ride until you find a height that works well. You may even stop several times during a ride to adjust your seat height: lower for swooping down hills, higher for pedaling on the flats and climbing.

out and look foolish. Instead of giving it everything you've got and pooping out halfway up, shift to a low gear, stay seated as long as pos-

sible, keep your upper body relaxed, and maintain a quick, steady cadence as you spin your way up. You may not be the first one to the

"I DID IT!"

Missouri's Berryman Trail, called "the best mountain bike spot between the Rockies and the Appalachians" by *Bike* magazine, is a 24-mile single-track loop built by the Civilian Conservation Corps in the 1930s. Its enticing switchbacks send you up hillsides in the most civilized way: Few of the climbs are steep enough to require walking. Two natural springs, a cave, numerous creek crossings, and a trail that skirts misty hollows keep things interesting.

Berryman has been there for me since I first began mountain biking. I've ridden it in every season, cleared windfall from ice storms, skinny-dipped in cool, spring-fed holes, and slept on its windy ridges. But until last summer, I'd never ridden the entire 24-mile length. Almost, but not quite. Forest roads bisecting the loop provide perfect bail-out opportunities along the trail, and I took advantage of them. Last summer, it was time. I would finish the Berryman.

The day I chose was hot, but by Missouri standards not terribly hot. Mid-eighties, maybe ninety on sunny hillsides. I had plenty of water, food, bug spray, and tools. I'd had lots of sleep and water the night before. I was ready.

At the trailhead, my boyfriend and I met a mountain biker who had recently moved from the East Coast. He'd bought a house in a small town in the middle of the best Ozarks riding country. Only

top, but you might be the only one who pedaled the whole way. And you will have learned a lot about good climbing technique.

DESCENDING

Descending steep or challenging hills can be an intimidating proposition for a beginning mountain biker. Women,

---

problem was, he'd met no one to ride with. Sure, he could ride with us! The Lonely Guy was on a tricked out, full suspension titanium, bike.

The first four miles were great; the low morning sun lit the trail with scattered light. The three of us took turns setting the pace and I felt strong and limber, like I could ride all day. I couldn't stop smiling. Nearing mile 8, however, things took a turn for the worse.

As the sun rose higher in the sky, the cool hollows turned steamy, my breakfast cereal wore off, and Mr. Titanium started getting on my nerves. For the last few miles, he'd been riding my tail. "Back off, man! You're making me nervous," I thought, but didn't say. I offered to let him ride ahead, but he declined. It felt like there were lead weights in my bike bag. The worst part was, we'd ridden only one-third of the trail. "I'm a wimp," I thought to myself. "Why did I ever consider myself a mountain biker? No way I can finish this trail."

A few more crybaby miles, a granola bar, and a splash of cold creek water on my face, and I started feeling better. Much better. By mile 16 I was a new woman with new energy and determination. Soon we met up with friends from work riding in the other direction. They were closing in on the trailhead and the end of their ride. Everyone looked haggard — everyone except Mike, the young bike assembler who was savoring a foot-long Subway sandwich pulled from his Camelbak. His friends looked on enviously, gnawing limp Powerbars.

With eight miles to go, feeling confident that I could finish the trail, my thoughts wandered. Muscle, bone, heart, and lungs were propelling me along this winding roller coaster through the woods; this wasn't so bad. In fact, it was the most beautiful, sublime thing I'd ever experienced.

I faltered a few more times, of course. At mile 19, where the grade steepens and becomes rocky. At mile 23, when I thought the end would never come. But I did it! I would do it again. And each time, the trail seems a little easier and more sublime.

On very steep descents, lower your center of gravity and shift your weight back by moving your butt behind and below the saddle.

get too extreme. We thought that stunts were stupid and pointless. When was the last time you saw a little girl catching big air off a ramp or riding out a wheelie on her bike?

While we may not have been raised (or genetically programmed) to have the same risk-taking, daredevilish tendencies as males, I'm living proof that these characteristics can be developed and nurtured in adulthood. A quiet, reserved young woman, I used to express my physical side through vigorous, yet relatively tame pursuits like aerobics and running. Now, although I'm a safe rider, I like nothing better than an exhilarating

especially, seem wary of this at first. When you think about how most girls grew up riding bikes as compared to boys, it's easy to see why we're a little freaked out about downhilling. We rode Barbie-pink bikes with silver tassels on the handlebars back and forth on the sidewalk, in the driveway, or to our friends' houses. Unlike the boys, who went tearing off homemade jumps, most of us didn't

---

TECHNIQUE TIP

TAKE A HIKE

Who says you always have to ride when riding? On extremely steep hills, the best thing to do may be to stop pedaling and start walking your bike. Even the world's best riders occasionally walk, including Juli Furtado, two-time world and four-time national mountain-biking champion. "Even in races, I'll sometimes get off and walk," says Furtado. "When it's really steep, walking is often the wisest thing to do to save energy."

Start descents at a slow speed and level your pedals for a solid platform to stand on as you move your weight back.

ride down a fast, rocky hill on my favorite trail. However, it took a lot of work to get to this point.

A few tips to remember as you're practicing descending:

● Don't start descents too fast. Start out slowly and build controllable speed as you go. If you start out too fast, you'll be more likely to hit the brakes and lose control.

❷ Level your pedals until they are parallel with the ground and form a platform for you to stand on. With the pedals levelled, they are less likely to catch on trail obstacles.

❸ Get off the saddle. Any time you

TECHNIQUE TIP
GET UP TO GET DOWN

"A critical thing about going downhill is to establish a low center of gravity," says Ned Overend, 1990 mountain-biking world champion. Ironically, the way to get your center of gravity lower is to stand up out of the saddle. By standing, most of your weight is on the pedals, while if you remain sitting, most of your weight rests higher up on the saddle.

Stream crossings are refreshing during a hot ride whether you stay aboard your bike or shoulder your load (below).

saddle. How far behind depends on how steep the hill is. On a slight downhill, keep your butt slightly behind the saddle. On a steep downhill, your butt should be way behind the saddle. Practice to find the right balance. Shifting your body weight over your rear tire gives you more traction and control of the bike.

⑤ Keeping your legs and arms bent and fairly loose allows them to absorb shock from the trail. At the same time, try to keep a strong, but not tense, grip on the handlebars.

⑥ Use your thighs to grip the sides of your saddle to help you keep the bike under control on bumpy descents.

⑦ Prior to descending, shift to the next largest chain ring to take up slack in the chain and give you some resistance, should you want to pedal. Just be prepared for the next rise or obstacle, when you'll want to be in a lower gear again.

descend, your butt should be off the saddle and you should be standing on the pedals.

④ Get your weight behind the

TECHNIQUE TIP

SHOULDERING THE LOAD

When slinging your bike over your shoulder—as mountain bikers must do from time to time—sling it over your right shoulder. That will keep the drivetrain away from your body, keeping your clothing free of chain grease and avoiding nasty scratches from the chain-ring teeth.

HOW TO FALL

If you're a mountain biker, you will fall. There's no getting around it. But that doesn't mean you'll always hurt yourself. Interestingly, the most severe cycling injuries I've witnessed have happened on, not off, the road. The mountain bikers I've known, particularly the beginners, tend to get scraped, bruised, and bumped often, but generally avoid the more serious injuries — dislocations, fractures, and deep cuts — of road cyclists. This is probably because mountain bikers travel more slowly, aren't competing for space with motor vehicles, and usually have a softer place to land than on pavement. You can prevent many serious injuries by learning the correct way to fall.

Your first instinct will probably be to stick your hands out to break the fall. If you're wearing good, tough gloves and are not moving very fast, you might escape with just a torn glove and a few bumps or bruises. But if you happen to land wrong, you could easily break a bone in your wrist. A better way to fall is to tuck and roll. In the split second you have before impact, look for the softest place with the least obstacles and aim for it. Then, instead of doing your Superman impression with arms outstretched, curl up into a ball and roll into the fall. The rolling motion allows the absorption of impact to be spread out over a greater area, rather than

The safest way to fall is to tuck and roll, avoiding the instinct to stick out your hands to absorb the fall.

concentrated in one small area of the body. And tucking your arms and legs close to your body protects both the limbs and the major organs housed in your torso. If possible, try to land clear of your bicycle to protect both it and you from more serious damage.

But there are times when the tuck-and-roll move is ill-advised. When falling on trails that skirt steep hillsides or drop off on one side, grab the nearest tree and hang on!

LOG CROSSING

Until fairly recently, I placed a lot of importance on log crossings. I thought my ability or inability to ride over logs of a certain size defined me as a mountain biker. But after riding with other women — including some racers — who avoided the same logs, I realized that I may have been setting unrealistic expectations by comparing myself to male mountain bikers who thrive on crossing bigger and bigger obstacles.

I don't mean to imply that women can't or shouldn't attempt to cross logs. It's important to challenge yourself, and hey, it's fun. I love logs now and miss them when I'm riding a super clean trail. However, I think that women should try to accept various definitions of "a successful ride" or "a good rider" and be open to the notion of riding pursued for pure enjoyment, not for comparison or competition with others, especially men.

That said, here's how to cross a log:

❶ Start with mere sticks, not logs. Once you're at ease with the motions

TECHNIQUE TIP

THE BUMP THRUST

The world is a bumpy place, and the world of mountain biking is often an incredibly bumpy place. Bumps, ranging from pavement seams on the road to logs across a trail, can be jarring interruptions at best and crash causers at worst. But there is a way of taking the jar out of the bump—call it the bump thrust.

of lifting your front wheel and unweighting your rear wheel to cross an object, you can gradually work up to larger logs.

🔵 Maintain enough speed to get over the log, but not so much that you lose control.

🔵 Just as you would if you were approaching any other bump, stand on your pedals and keep your knees and arms loose and bent to absorb shock.

🔵 When you get to the log, shift your weight slightly back, lift the front wheel, roll it up onto the log and down the other side. Then shift your weight forward to unweight the rear wheel. If you forget this last part, your rear wheel will slam into the log, possibly resulting in a flat tire or a dented rim. Ideally, this becomes a linked series of fluid motions.

🔵 When you see a log lying at a weird angle in the trail, try to approach it at a 90-degree angle to make crossing easier.

🔵 Practice. I like to go to my favorite local trail early in the morning with my riding buddy, pick an open spot where we can build up speed, and

---

The bump thrust is a way of pushing and throwing—*thrusting*—the bike over a bump. When you see a bump ahead, stop pedaling and allow yourself to feel light in the saddle. For a particularly large bump, you might want to stand up on the pedals to help absorb the jolt. As you approach the bump, give a quick push to the handlebars to accelerate the front wheel and lighten its load, helping it to roll smoothly over the bump.

As you get good at this technique, you can add lift to it for larger obstacles. (1) As you lurch your body back, simultaneously yank up on the handlebars. As the front wheel clears the log (2), move your body forward to help the rear wheel over, but make sure not to grab the front brakes in the process. Now, with your weight centered (3), keep up your momentum by giving a push on the pedals.

practice crossing progressively larger logs. You can also do this in your backyard or a park near your house.

SOFT SURFACES

Part of the beauty of mountain biking is that you encounter all kinds of plants, animals, and terrain that you'd never see if you were riding on the road. Different natural trail surfaces demand their own special body language to clear — loose gravel, hardpacked dirt, deep sand, slippery mud. To ride through soft stuff, get in a low gear, shift your weight to the rear, and spin your way through. Get accustomed to how it feels when your rear wheel is dancing around in loose terrain. Another tip: If you're having difficulty riding on a muddy trail, that should tell you something. Leave and come back later when conditions are drier.

Sometimes a wet, muddy trail should be taken as a message to turn around and ride another, drier, day.

HITTING
THE
TRAIL

You have the bike, the gear, and the will to ride. Now what? Go do it! There are paved bike paths, gravel roads, rail-trails, backcountry single-track, and more to choose from. Two pieces of advice: Start off easy and move up to more challenging trails as you gain skills and confidence. And don't begin even the easiest ride without preparing.

A lack of adequate planning on my first serious mountain biking trip was nearly enough to put me off mountain biking for good, despite the best intentions of everyone involved. My boyfriend and I thought we had planned well. We'd purchased a guidebook of local mountain bike trails and chosen one listed as "great for both beginning and experienced riders." We had water, tools, and bug repellent. I'd even thought ahead enough to leave a bag of raisins and peanuts in the car for after the ride when we'd be hungry.

Fourteen miles, two flat tires, and five hours later, we raced darkness back to the trailhead. I use the word "raced" loosely. Near the end, I no longer had the energy or the desire to ride, and trudged along the trail pushing my bike and cursing every rock, stick, and spider web in my path.

Where did we go wrong? The distance was much too long for my

NO MOTORIZE
VEHICLES, AT
OR HORSES
ON TRAIL

fitness level. Fourteen miles might have been fine for a beginner on a gentle rail-trail, but not on that rough backcountry trail. We should have read the trail description more closely, noted the author's references to "rocky and technical climbs," and waited to tackle this unfamiliar trail until I was a more seasoned rider. Even the food was not quite right. Rather than the fat and protein of peanuts, we could have used the quick energy of a cookie or granola bar. And the food I brought did us no good sitting in the car when we needed it on the trail.

Luckily, I recovered from my low blood sugar and bad attitude quickly after a much-needed meal, and went on to explore and enjoy shorter, less challenging trails in the following weeks.

Opposite: On the open trail, cycling along a bike trail in the Lake McBride State Park north of Iowa City, Iowa. Above: Respect trail-use signs and all those you encounter on the trail.

WHERE TO RIDE

Perhaps the best place to start the discussion of where to ride is where not to ride. Bikes are prohibited in any of the designated wilderness areas across the United States. State parks, national parks, urban parks, and county parks may also limit use, particularly on overused trails in need of rehabilitation. Even trails that look as if they'd be perfect for riding may be off-limits to bikes. A rule allowing equestrians, but not mountain bikers, on wilderness trails has confounded me for years. But, no matter how tempting it is, don't ride in areas closed to mountain bikes. If you're not sure, call the agency that manages the land before you venture out.

So with all these prohibitions, where *can* you ride? Plenty of places. Many city, county, and state parks do allow bikes on trails and these are great places for learning to ride. Some are quite popular, so watch for others on the trail and be prepared to pay a small fee. My favorite places to ride — national forests — allow mountain bikes on gravel roads and most trails, and offer the scenic views and solitude that I crave. State recreation and conservation area trails are usually open to bikes, as are most

Pausing for a closer look at a petroglyph panel, Dinosaur National Monument, near the Utah-Colorado border.

IMBA AND RESPONSIBLE RIDING

The International Mountain Bicycling Association (IMBA) was created in 1988 as a coalition of mountain bike clubs determined to fight unwarranted trail closures by encouraging responsible riding and advocacy. More than a decade later, they're still at it. Thanks to their efforts, many of the best trails are open and in good condition.

IMBA Board President Ashley Korenblat puts it succinctly: "Our sport can't exist without public land. If you ride a bike off-road, you have a responsibility to help protect public land by riding appropriately."

You can reach the Boulder, Colorado–based group at (303) 545-9011, imba@aol.com or www.imba.com.

IMBA's Rules of the Trail

1. Ride on open trails only.
2. Leave no trace.
3. Control your bicycle.
4. Always yield the trail to other users.
5. Never scare animals.
6. Plan ahead.

Exploring Vermont's Northeast Kingdom. Ask permission to ride on private property and always re-close livestock gates behind you.

areas specifically designed for off-road vehicles. Ski areas generally allow mountain bikes on the slopes in the off-season, and many resorts are attracting new clients with well-groomed biking trails. In the west, Bureau of Land Management areas are open to bikes.

If you're not into single-track, you can find many lovely rides that are off the beaten path with a good map showing county or township roads. Pedaling these paved, gravel, or dirt backroads, you might see a field of sunflowers, grazing cows, or wild blackberries. Rail-trails and canal or levee paths provide a smooth surface and easy grades, and offer a good way to view waterways and old railroad towns.

For help finding places to ride, check out some of the numerous guidebooks on the market. The authors of these books, which may focus on single-track, gravel, or paved cycling routes, know their locales well and include everything from trail mileage to recommendations for a good mid-ride snack stop. You can find cycling guidebooks in bike stores and the local-interest or sports section of many bookstores. Maps and trail information can also be provided by national and state park headquarters and ranger stations.

Finding Your Way

In our society, women carry the unfortunate stereotype of lacking innate navigational abilities. This is baloney, of course. Women are just as capable as men of finding their way around, whether in the urban jungle or the dense forest. However, some women, young and old, have become comfortable with this stereotype, relying on others to navigate, doubting their own instincts, and neglecting to develop the skills required to move confidently through the countryside. I admit to being one of these women. Although I love looking at maps and pride myself on my ability to find my way around any city, until recently, I relied on my boyfriend to navigate in the back-country. I regret that I waited so long to learn these skills myself. It's incredibly empowering to find your own way.

Never venture out on unfamiliar trails without a map and compass. Trail maps are usually available at trailheads and park offices. Call or write ahead of time to acquire the necessary maps. On well-marked trails, navigating is usually just a matter of paying attention to the map, trail blazes, and your progress on the trail. Don't assume that just because you're following an open

MINIMIZING TRAIL DAMAGE

Any person, animal, or vehicle that travels a trail has the potential to leave its mark. Some things, like horses and motorized vehicles, leave more of an impression than others, and can do real damage to the trail and mess it up for other users. Mountain bikes too have some impact on trails, particularly in heavily used areas. But there are ways to ride that minimize trail damage and, ultimately, preserve our right to use the trails.

❶ Don't ride mushy, mucky trails. Wait until they dry out. Riding through mud causes ruts which act as erosion trenches. These ruts are extremely bothersome for other users.

❷ Keep your bike on the trail. Constantly running off the side of the trail erodes the trail edge.

❸ Keep your back wheel turning. Locking up your rear wheel while going down hills shreds the trail surface, causing erosion.

❹ Ride corners cleanly, without sliding. Sliding causes lateral erosion of the trail surface.

❺ Ride, or walk, over obstacles like roots and rocks, not around them. Riding around obstacles widens the trail and causes erosion.

Thanks to Roger McGehee for this information from his Web site, "Roger's Hints for Beginning Singletrackers: Suggestions for Minimizing Trail Conflicts." rogm@microweb.com

trail, it's the correct one. Natural areas can contain numerous intersecting trails and roads. If you haven't seen a trail marker in a while, retrace your steps to make sure you're on the correct trail. Pay attention to the time, your pace, your direction of travel, and the mileage you've covered to help you estimate when you will finish a trail ride. This is where a cyclocomputer comes in handy (See Chapter 2).

If you plan to ride backcountry trails, know how to use a topographical (such as a United States Geological Survey) map and a compass. Backcountry trails frequently intersect with jeep trails, animal paths, and gravel roads. Sometimes the trail simply fizzles out or becomes

Lending a hand, Western Spirit Cycling tour, Canyonlands National Park, Utah.

WHERE CAN I FIND WOMEN TO RIDE WITH?

● Hunt for WOMBATS. The Women's Mountain Bike and Tea Society is a nationwide network started by ex–pro racer Jacquie Phelan to build interest in and support for women's mountain biking. In addition to regular group rides led by WOMBATS members around the country, the group holds an annual jamboree in Durango, Colorado, where women come together to meet and learn riding skills and

bike maintenance and repair.

● Join the club. Local bike clubs and trail maintenance organizations are a great way to meet women who ride. In St. Louis, Missouri, the Women's Riding Network, for example, has a ride list containing the names and phone numbers of more than 150 local women cyclists. Network founder Margo Carroll leads group rides and publishes a quarterly newsletter with news about members and updated ride lists.

continued on page 100

continued from page 99

● Go to camp. Some bike shops, touring companies, and resorts offer women's mountain bike skill camps or classes where you can improve your technique in a comfortable, supportive environment and meet other gals who ride.

● Take a tour. Women-only bike tours are becoming more popular. Touring companies transport women, their bikes and camping equipment to trails in places like Utah, Idaho, and West Virginia.

● Seek the Summit. Bicycle manufacturer Specialized held its first Women's Cycling Summit in Palo Alto, California in 1998 to encourage and support women's cycling. The Summit was so popular that the company decided to conduct a series of them across the country in subsequent years. Besides meeting other women cyclists from their area, Summit participants can listen to guest speakers on topics like nutrition, fitness, and bicycle technology; participate in group rides; learn mountain biking technique; and check out new cycling products.

● Head to the bike shop. Ask the staff for names of women who ride, post a "Seeking Women Riding Partners" flyer on their bulletin board, or place a classified ad in a local outdoor interest magazine.

● Talk to women at the trailhead. Although Angie Sheehy is usually reserved, when she saw another woman pedaling her favorite trail four years ago, she struck up a conversation. Now the two are good friends and frequent riding partners.

● Try a race. You don't have to be a world-class athlete. Even for those brand-new to mountain biking, racing is a great way to develop skills, improve your self-confidence, meet other women riders, and have fun. Most race series offer opportunities for beginning, intermediate, and advanced mountain bikers. The National Off-Road Bicycle Association sanctions races around the country and offers categories designated as Beginner, Sport, Expert, and Pro.

See "Sources & Resources" for more information.

impassable. Choosing an appropriate detour or shortcut, or finding your way back if you become lost, requires map and compass skills.

These items, together with a small flashlight, have saved me several times when I was caught out on the trail after dark.

Seek out women's bicycling networks. Riding with other women can help you gain confidence and learn new skills.

WHO TO RIDE WITH
Riding With Women

When I began mountain biking, I rode exclusively with my boyfriend, who'd introduced me to the sport. While I loved the time we spent together, I longed to find some women riding partners. Unfortunately, I had no idea where to look, since I rarely saw other women on the rugged trails we favored.

One day, while leafing through a local outdoor magazine, I saw an ad for a women's bicycling network. Several months later I went for a group mountain bike ride. I wish it hadn't taken me so long. Riding with other women helped me gain confidence in my riding skills as a beginner and presented a wonder-fully different way of enjoying the sport. Instead of huffing and puffing to keep up I could take part in conversation and good-natured teasing, and once I made it to the top of a climb I could enjoy the view without berating myself for being a slowpoke.

Other women share similar experiences. Cyndi Weiss, of Fenton, Missouri, began riding a mountain bike 12 years ago while on whitewater kayaking trips with a club she and her husband belonged to. While her husband and the other men braved some extra-challenging river rapids, Weiss and several other women in the club sought out the local single-track for adventures of their own.

"I got to the point where I looked

biking spots in North Carolina, West Virginia, and Utah at least twice a year. Attending group rides sponsored by a women's cycling club keeps her connected with local women who like to ride.

Having mountain biked with both women and men, Weiss has observed differences in how each tends to approach the sport.

"The men seem to go out with the intention of improving their skills and their

A mountain biking couple enjoying the trails on Jekyll Island, Georgia.

forward to the mountain biking more than the kayaking. I love it — covering ground, seeing the wildlife and terrain," says Weiss.

Over the years, Weiss has introduced several friends and neighbors to the joys of mountain biking. Now Weiss, with her husband or her girlfriends, travels to favorite mountain times. They're much more competitive. Women tend to use mountain biking as a way to see and enjoy their surroundings and be with friends. Most women have a more social, laid-back approach to the sport."

Weiss believes mountain biking's reputation as an extreme, male-dominated sport keeps some women from pursuing or enjoying it.

"It scares some women off, and among women who do ride, I think if more got out there and just rode at their own pace they'd enjoy it more. Some women are so concerned about keeping up with or impressing the guys that they lose sight of why they're out there — to have fun."

Ashley Korenblat concurs, to a point, but thinks women shouldn't dismiss men as riding partners. Korenblat is president of both the International Mountain Bicycling Association and Western Spirit Cycling, a bike touring company based in Moab, Utah.

"Women are so worried about making guys wait on rides. But what they don't realize is that usually guys love having girls along; it gives them a good excuse to take more breaks. My advice to women is, go for it. Stop worrying and have fun."

Riding With Men

Mountain biking can also be a great way to spend time with the guys in your life — husband, lover, brother, father, or friend — and many women are introduced to the sport by a male. Whether you're exploring a rugged trail with map and compass or taking a leisurely spin on a paved path, pedaling trails together has a way of creating awesome memories.

One day in October, 1997, my boyfriend and I set out early in the morning to ride 13 miles of single-

If you're having trouble keeping up with a stronger rider, offer to take the lead so you can set the pace.

track encircling a small lake in Missouri's Mark Twain National Forest. The trail had recently been completed and this was our first time exploring it. Snaking along the shoreline on that crisp, cloudy day, the single-track spirits smiled on us. We picked our way along a trail as knotted and gnarled as a witch's hand, swooped down steep limestone chutes, and ended a long, hard climb with the discovery of an old, moss-covered stone schoolhouse. Nearing the end of our ride atop a large earthen dam, we braced ourselves against strong gusts coming off the lake and peered over the side at the misty valley below. Neither of us

♀

WOMAN-TO-WOMAN

IT'S YOUR RIDE

"Some men advise me, 'You should keep a training log,' or 'You should try to ride more obstacles,' but those are their goals, not mine. What I love about mountain biking is being in the woods, being active, exploring. I'm not out there to prove anything."

Cyndi Weiss, postal clerk,
House Springs, Missouri

could think of any place in the world we'd rather be.

Mountain biking with men can have drawbacks, though. Physiological differences between men and women are a fact of life. Most women have significantly less aerobic capacity, less overall body strength, a greater percentage of body fat, and a lower ratio of strength to weight than most men. These differences can make for friction or hurt feelings on the trail if a man's performance and expectations on a bike ride greatly surpass those of his female riding partner.

If you're having trouble keeping up with the guys on rides:

● Offer to ride at the front of the pack so you set the pace.

● Don't start out riding as fast as you can. You'll only get worn out quickly. Warm up by riding at an easy pace and speed up gradually.

● Learn the shortcuts. At my favorite single-track trail, I can use forest roads to cut the 24-mile loop

into shorter loops, depending on my energy level.

● If there's a possibility that you'll be left behind on a ride, be prepared. Bring a trail map, compass, snack, water, and tools for minor repairs.

● Don't take it personally. Make the most of your ride by yourself. If you're getting left behind by your riding partners regularly, ride with someone closer to your skill level.

Angie Sheehy works as a mechanic and salesperson in a bike shop and meets mountain bikers every day. However, she has a difficult time finding women who will ride the rugged off-road trails she likes. As a result, she mountain bikes with a group of men in their early 20s who work in her shop.

"They're great guys, it's a lot of fun, and I challenge myself riding with them because I have to push myself to keep up. But there are disadvantages, the main one being that they always have to be first. I guess it's a blow to their egos to be passed by a gal. And it's interesting to see the differences. Even though skill-wise, I'm probably a better technical rider than they are, there's a big strength difference. They can use raw power to get up hills and over obstacles, while I have to make sure I pick the right line."

But Michele Keane cautions women, especially beginners, against mountain biking solely with men.

"One thing that can hold women back as mountain bikers is always riding with and comparing themselves to men. If a woman's only basis for comparison on the trail is a group of guys she rides with, she may never measure up and, as a result, she'll get down on herself and get a twisted view of her own skills. I hear women mountain bikers,

Solitude in God's country: A lone mountain biker camps in southern Utah's Valley of the Gods.

even racers, say it all the time: 'I suck.' Riding with other women from time to time tends to bring things back into perspective."

Riding Alone

Before the 1890s, social restrictions discouraged women from riding bicycles alone. Chaperones, corsets, and beliefs suggesting that cycling by oneself was (for females) immoral, unfeminine, and unhealthy kept most women off bicycles. But by the early 1900s, women realized the bicycle could be a tool to help them leave these kinds of restrictions behind. Cycling helped women achieve greater independence and they took to the sport by the thousands. Today,

millions of women own bikes, and while fears of mechanical breakdowns or harassment may keep some of them from cycling alone, others treasure the solitude and self-confidence gained.

"Riding alone has benefits that I don't get anywhere else," says Margo Carroll. "It's my time to think, to explore ideas and crazy dreams. And since I rarely see other people in the woods — usually just hikers or other mountain bikers — I feel more secure there than I do on the road."

Your first solo mountain bike ride can be intimidating, until you do it. Stephanie Ashley, a middle-school art teacher, relates her experience:

A rider enjoys a spring morning, Cedar Lake Trail, Shawnee National Forest, southeast Illinois.

"I had always ridden with my husband, but one day he wasn't available and I wanted to ride. So I packed up my bike and gear and drove out to the trailhead for an all-day ride by myself. Trusting my own skills and instincts, and discovering that I could do it, was an incredibly powerful feeling and it's opened up the possibility of new adventures for me. Now, I'm planning a solo wilderness camping trip. "

Although city riding is very different, Rio Hall, a community activist, also enjoys cycling alone in her hometown of St. Louis. Hall rides her bike, a Specialized Rockhopper fitted with slick tires, to work, to the grocery store, and to visit friends. Riding alone in the city, a woman must use common sense and decide for herself what feels safe. Although Hall carries pepper spray and has studied self-defense techniques, she believes a large part of feeling safe alone on a bike in the city is attitude and awareness. Familiarity with your surroundings and acting in a self-confident manner contribute more to safety than any weapon you could carry, Hall says.

"Nothing is completely safe. But I'm not going to live in fear. I'm going to protect myself as much as possible, and I'm going to do what I want."

Riding alone, whether in the city or the wilds, makes ordinary precautions even more important: Carry bike tools and know how to use them. Let someone know where you're going and when you expect to return. Be familiar with the trail and carry a map and compass. Some women feel safer looking androgenous on solo rides; they tuck long hair into their helmet and wear baggy, nondescript clothing. Some like to carry a cellular phone for emergencies.

For additional tips on safety when riding alone, see Chapter 8, "Make the Most of Your Ride."

Mother and daughter enjoy each other's company along a carriage road in Acadia National Park, Maine.

Riding With Children

Karen Johnson, a mother and mountain bike racer, says pulling her two young children in the Burley trailer behind her bike is "the best workout I've ever had, and a blast for the kids." Freed from concerns about traffic, Johnson feels confident taking Reid, six, and Katie, four, on up to 14-mile rides on an urban paved bike path. As long as it's not too hot and they have plenty to entertain them, Reid and Katie love it too. Off-road adventures in a county park are fun as well, but the Johnsons have learned to be cautious around the equestrians who share the dirt trails.

"We nearly had a catastrophe with a horse who was terrified of the trailer. He reared back on his hind legs and his eyes got really wide. Finally the kids started talking. Once the horse heard their voices and knew there were people inside the trailer, he calmed down."

An active, outdoorsy family that also skis and hikes, the Johnsons are already thinking about how to get Reid and Katie comfortable with riding their bikes off-road. "We encourage them to ride their bikes in the grass, not just on the sidewalk, so they learn how to handle a bike in a

TIPS FOR RIDING WITH YOUNG CHILDREN

● Never attempt challenging off-road trails with a small child in tow. Stick to paved bike paths, rail-trail conversions, low-traffic gravel roads, neighborhood streets, or gentle dirt trails.

● Avoid child seats carried on the bike. They can easily throw you off balance, making bike handling unpredictable and falls more likely. Opt for a pull-behind trailer instead.

● Pulling a trailer and child behind your bike can add as much as 80 pounds to your load. As a result, you pick up more speed when decending hills. Slow down when going around turns, as this extra speed could cause the trailer to tip.

● Make riding with your kids part of your training routine. Pulling their extra weight in the trailer makes even small hills a great workout and they'll enjoy it too, but be flexible. Stop every half hour or so to play, walk around, or have a snack.

● Always wear a helmet when you ride. Children whose parents set a good example are likely to follow their lead. Helmets are available for infants as young as six months old and are crucial

safety equipment, even if the child is enclosed in a trailer. In addition, protect your child's eyes with sunglasses, skin with sunscreen or clothing, and feet with shoes.

● When a child outgrows her trailer or child seat, but is still too little for her own bike, consider using a trailer bike that attaches to the rear of a parent's bike or a family tandem.

● Look for trailers and kids' bikes in bright colors and make use of safety flags to boost visibility.

way that's easy, safe, and not intimidating. And even though they're still on training wheels, we plan to take them to ride some easy dirt trails this fall."

However, Johnson says she won't be buying her kids miniature mountain bikes with gears and shocks anytime soon. "Reid is interested in BMX and I'm going to encourage that. It looks like so much fun; they're out with other kids, and they develop great bike-handling skills. Most of the adult mountain bike racers I admire started out in BMX racing."

Matt Sheehy, eight, began riding a seven-mile off-road trail, single-track and all, with his parents when he was six. While mom Angie is a gung-ho mountain biker, she would never have attempted such a trip had Matt not suggested it himself.

"I didn't want to push him into doing something just because I like to do it. But when he asked to go, I said, 'Sure.' Once we were out there, he didn't want to quit. He fell a few times, but didn't get hurt. It was a good experience and we've returned to do the trail a few times since."

Sheehy believes her own enthusiasm about bikes is one reason Matt is eager. "Sometimes I'll practice riding wheelies and bunny hopping out in the yard and the next day, I'll see him out there trying it." Sheehy and her husband started Matt out on a bike with training wheels when he was five. The training wheels came off when he was six, and last year he graduated from a 20-inch BMX bike to a 24-inch Trek kid's mountain bike. It took Matt about two months to get comfortable with the bike's

NIGHT RIDE

The crisp November air chills me quickly as I move away from the campfire. I am one member of a village of mountain bikers at North Carolina's Tsali Recreation Area that has settled in for the night, with firewood stacked, tent erected, and Coleman lantern glowing.

The more comfortable I become next to the fire, the less likely I am to fulfill my promise to go night riding with my friend. So I get up, crawl into the tent, and change into cycling garb: tights, wool socks, long-sleeved jersey, fleece pullover, and lined gloves. I strap my rechargeable light to my helmet, and stuff my battery pack into my CamelBak, and we begin pedaling the gravel road that leads from the campground to the trail. Since I know there are black bear in the Smokies, and

continued on page 110

continued from page 109

it's in our best interest not to scare one, my friend Steph and I decide to keep our conversation constant throughout the ride. We ride more slowly than we do in the daytime so we can talk and spot trail dropoffs in plenty of time to stop. Since Steph's bike is outfitted with two lights to my one, I follow her lead on the narrow single-track.

Tsali's six-mile Mouse Branch Loop Trail is perfect for night riding. Its smooth, hardpacked surface traverses gently rolling hills skirting several inlets of Fontana Lake. At the beginning, we snake up the side of the mountain and see the glow of a dozen fires in the campground below. In the valley, we can make out our own camp and even the shadow of our friend who is rummaging inside her tent.

The trail looks eerie as we follow the narrow beams from our bike lights through the darkness. I see lights flickering in the woods ahead. Although I know they're just the lights of other mountain bikers enjoying the woods at night, their entry into our dark solitude makes me shiver.

At a clearing in the trail we decide to take a break. With our lights out, we can see the black outline of the tall peaks in Great Smoky Mountain National Park looming across the lake. Above us, the full moon is rising against a backdrop of a thousand stars.

"You ready to get going?" I ask.

"Sure. I'm starting to get chilled," Steph says.

As we clip into our pedals and prepare to turn on our lights again, we see a flash of green light slice through the sky. A firework? A safety flare? A shooting star? We're not sure. But it certainly added to the mystery and wonder of our night ride on the Mouse Branch Trail.

gearing, hand brakes, and slightly larger size, but now he's a pro.

Riding With a Dog
Taking your dog to run alongside you on a trail or abandoned dirt road offers fun, companionship, and a feeling of security on a backcountry ride. Adrienne Murphy started her dog Kiko on short two-mile runs to get him in shape for their six- to ten-mile mountain bike rides.

"He absolutely loves it. He does best on tight single-track because it slows the riders down so he can keep up easily. He wears his little doggie backpack and carries our PowerBars and a plastic bag full of dog food, and he drinks right out of my water bottle. I think mountain biking and camping with a dog makes sense for a woman, since people are less likely to bother her if she has a dog," Murphy says. When riding with a dog, keep in mind:

There is no better way to tire out an energetic dog than to bring him along on a ride. Do so only if your dog is well trained.

● Not everyone welcomes dogs on the trail. Check to see that dogs are allowed where you plan to ride. Never take a dog on a busy urban trail, even if there's no posted prohibition.

● Can your dog mind his manners? Are you confident he'll behave in a civilized, non-threatening way when he encounters other dogs or people on the trail? If not, leave him at home.

● Make sure your dog is up to the challenge. Limit your ride time, pace, and distance to what he can comfort- ably handle and keep a close eye on how he's doing. If Fido normally spends his time flopped on the floor with a chew toy, taking him on a vig- orous ride could endanger his health.

● Bring plenty of water and a small plastic bowl. Don't assume that your dog will drink out of your CamelBak. Ride near natural bodies of water so he can drink up or jump in to cool off.

Time out to read the map along Lolo Trail in northern Idaho, part of Lewis and Clark's 1805–06 route.

● Protect his feet. Running on rough trails, the pads of a dog's feet can get cut or bruised. Several companies make dog booties with Cordura uppers, Velcro closures, and leather or synthetic soles to keep doggie's feet pain-free.

● If you ride where hunters, equestrians, bears, or mountain lions are a possibility, make sure your dog wears a band of orange fabric and/or a collar with bells to announce his presence. Surprising a hunter or a wild animal isn't safe.

● If your dog wears a pack, make sure it weighs no more than one-third his body weight when full.

● Don't let your dog do his business on the trail. If he does, use some sticks or leaves to pick it up and bury it in a small hole off-trail.

FITNESS
AND
NUTRITION

Mountain biking is an excellent way to stay healthy and fit. It doesn't stress the bones and joints with the constant pounding of running or aerobics. It builds lower-body muscular strength and endurance, and hones your agility and balance. And according to professional triathlete and Ironman champion Paula Newby-Fraser — one of the fittest women in the world — mountain biking's climbing and high gear turnover make it a superior cardiovascular conditioner. In fact, in her book, *Peak Fitness for Women,* Newby-Fraser says she'd prefer to spend less time riding the roads on her ultralight, sleek triathlon bike and more time training with her mountain bike on off-road trails. The interesting surroundings and exciting terrain keeps training from becoming a bore, she says.

As with any exercise, the more vigorously and regularly you work out, the more benefits you will realize. However, part of the beauty of mountain biking is that you can ride fast or slow, on steep, technical terrain or gently rolling gravel roads, and still feel the benefits. It's so much fun your "workout time" will fly by whether you ride for a half hour or all day long.

♀

BIKING FOR FITNESS

"Nine years ago when I 'retired' from tennis because of a knee problem, I was looking for a knee-friendly sport that would keep me in great shape. I found it in mountain biking. I can ride for hours on the smooth, fast terrain we have around here. But mountain biking represents many things beyond just fitness for me: stress relief, a sense of accomplishment and independence. It truly is a lifetime sport."

Isabel Dickson, mountain bike instructor,
Bryson City, North Carolina

TRAINING FOR PERFORMANCE AND FITNESS

If you're serious about training and improving your fitness through mountain biking, you may want to begin measuring your heart rate, which is the number of beats per minute. Mountain bikers usually like to do this with a heart rate monitor worn on the body, rather than taking the pulse at the wrist or neck which requires removing the hands from the handlebars.

To increase your aerobic capacity and fitness level, you must exercise in your target heart rate range (60–80 percent of your maximum heart rate) for at least 20 minutes at a time. The standard formula for estimating your maximum heart rate is 220 minus your age. For a more accurate measurement of your personal maximum heart rate, and, therefore, your target range, consider taking a treadmill stress test at a doctor's office or sports medicine center.

CROSS-TRAINING AND RECOVERY FOR TOTAL WELL-BEING

When I first began mountain biking on challenging trails, I was sore a lot. I'd fall and bang up my elbows, strain my knees on climbs, or knot up my neck muscles from tensing them all the time. That's when I began to see the value in a well-rounded exercise routine that included recovery days.

Instead of just riding trails all the time, I started swimming one day a week. Several mornings I would get up early to do some strength training exercises before work — ab crunches, pushups, arm curls — or go for a walk around my neighborhood. On Friday evenings after work, I attended a yoga class where I learned stretching, deep breathing, and relaxation techniques.

It worked! My body recovered more quickly from falls and I could bike harder and longer without all the aches and pains. I still stretch and take recovery days. I also enjoy occasional studio cycling (spinning) classes, jogs in the park, and weekend backpacking or canoe trips. Even my short four-mile ride to work has improved my speed and endurance on the trail considerably.

Keep your activities varied, listen to your body's cues, and take occasional no-exercise days to achieve better performance on the trail and keep your body fully fit and pain-free.

STRENGTH TRAINING

Many active women have strong thigh and buttock muscles that assist them immensely in mountain biking.

HEALTHY LIFESTYLE

"For me, mountain biking has been symbiotic with quitting smoking. I smoked for 10 years, but when I started biking, I began to see just how much of a detriment it was. Becoming a better rider was part of my motivation for quitting. It's amazing now to go up hills without pain."

Stephanie Ashley, art teacher,
Hillsboro, Missouri

LOOSENING UP TO RIDE

Before hitting the road or trail, a full stretching regimen is great—if you can squeeze 15 to 20 minutes of stretching time into a tight schedule. If you can't, even five minutes of stretching can yield a big pay-off when it comes to how long and painlessly you can ride.

If you can afford only an abbreviated stretching routine, concentrate on the muscles that typically are put under the most duress during a ride: the quadriceps, the hamstrings, the muscles of the lower back, and the neck muscles. The following stretches are designed for that purpose. For the definitive guide to stretching for all sports and activities, see *Stretching,*

by Bob Anderson.

Before you start contorting your body in the ways suggested in these drawings, keep in mind a few guidelines:

● Try to hold each position 15 to 30 seconds.

● Don't bounce or jerk. Stretch as far as you can in an easy and relaxed manner.

● Never stretch to the point where it hurts, only to the point where the muscles feel tight.

● If you've got time, do the same stretching routine after riding.

NECK & SPINE
Sit on the floor with your right leg straight. Cross your left foot over your right knee and rest

continued on page 116

continued from page 115

it on the floor. Then rest your right elbow on the outside of your left knee. Now, with your left hand resting on the floor behind you, slowly turn your head to look over your left shoulder.

HAMSTRINGS & LOWER BACK

Sitting on the ground or floor, tuck your right foot into your groin. Straighten your left leg and reach as far forward as you can. Hold that position, then change to the other leg.

QUADRICEPS

Bracing yourself against a wall with your right hand, grab your right foot with your left hand and raise the leg as far as you can without cramping or pain. Now change to the other leg.

CALF & ACHILLES TENDON

Bracing yourself against a wall with one hand over the other, and your feet about 2 feet from the wall, bring your right leg forward and bend it at the knee. Moving your torso toward the wall, gently extend the calf and Achilles tendon of your left leg, keeping your left foot flat on the floor. Now change to the other leg.

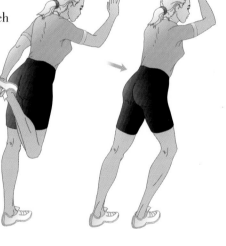

However, it is the rare woman who has strong arm, shoulder, and abdomen muscles. As a result, women sometimes have difficulty with important aspects of mountain biking, like effectively controlling the bike's front end. Climbing hills that are steep, long, or contain obstacles keeps the upper- and mid-body muscles active, and if the muscles are not up to the challenge, they tire quickly. Descending long or rocky hills, manuevering through rough terrain, and carrying the bike also puts hand, arm, and shoulder muscles to the test. Advanced skills like log crossing, bunny hopping, and wheelies are virtually impossible without a strong upper body.

Some of this is physiological. On average, women have approximately 56 percent of the upper body strength of men, according to Christine Wells, author of *Women, Sport, and Perfomance: A Physiological Perspective*. Women generally have fewer and smaller muscle fibers and a higher percentage of body fat than men. Where men can muscle through a tough section of trail, women may falter.

Strength training is the obvious solution, but some women are still reluctant to do resistance exercises for fear of developing big muscles. They needn't worry. Women have the ability to make large gains in strength without building bulky muscles as men do. According to Wells, the inability of women to gain significant muscle mass, even while they make substantial strength improvements, is due to their relatively low level of testosterone. Even a woman who lifts the heaviest weights is not

Ten to fifteen minutes of stretches before riding is great, but even a five-minute stretch will make a big difference.

likely to bulk up her physique unless she is taking anabolic steriods.

So why not make the most of what nature gave you? A little strength training makes a big difference in your performance on the trail. After I started doing just 40 pushups every other day, I found I was able to

?

DID YOU KNOW

Braking requires strong hands. According to *Women's Sports and Fitness*, pro mountain bike racer Shari Kain strengthens her hands by doing gripping exercises with hand strengtheners . . . you know, those things with the springs you squeeze.

bunny hop and work my way up rooty, rocky hillsides much more easily. In her book *Training for Cycling*, Olympic cycling champ Connie Carpenter recommends a three-times-a-week weight training routine and active, upper-body sports like cross-country skiing, swimming, and rock climbing to improve overall strength.

Pro mountain-bike racer Michele Kean, a certified personal trainer, strengthens her arms, wrists, shoulders, and back muscles by doing pullups, wrist curls, and bicep curls. A seated rowing machine helps further strengthen her shoulder muscles. Eco-Challenge veteran Adrienne Murphy says the good, old-fashioned, full-extension pushup is one of the best ways for a woman to build strong arms and shoulders. "I hate that 'girl pushup' crap," Murphy says. "If a woman has sufficient abdominal strength to keep her back flat, rather than swayed, she should be doing a full pushup, not those wimpy things that start at the knees."

Another strength exercise helpful for women mountain bikers is the abdominal crunch or sit-up. Crunches help banish the lower back pain that women frequently suffer (and that can be aggravated by biking) by strengthening the abdominal muscles that mountain biking tends to neglect. Done regularly, they also develop the flat stomach that many women admire. To do crunches, lie on the floor and bend both legs until your feet are flat on the floor. Put your hands behind your head and lift your head, neck, and shoulders off the floor. Don't forget to breathe; exhale up, inhale down. Try to complete 100 to 150 crunches in a session, three times a week.

A little activity to warm your muscles is smart prior to strength training, mountain biking, or any other strenuous exercise. Run in place for a few minutes or do 50 jumping jacks to warm up. Don't do strength exercises every day. Your muscles need time to rest and rebuild after a training session. Strength training three times a week should be plenty to build the strength you need to become a stronger mountain biker.

THE POWER OF WATER

According to exercise physiologists, our bodies need approximately eight ounces of water for every 30 minutes of vigorous exercise, as well as more water before and after the activity.

If you're new to mountain biking, it's easy to get stuck out on a ride, miles from nowhere, with no water. Luckily, it's just as easy to avoid the problem by planning ahead. Following are some tips about water I've learned through experience on the trail:

Don't wait until you're thirsty to take a drink; make a habit of doing so regularly.

● Don't wait until you feel thirsty to drink. By that time, you're probably slightly dehydrated. Even if you're not thirsty, drink small amounts of water frequently. When you urinate, your urine should look clear or very light-yellow. If it's darker, you're on the road to dehydration.

● You need more than you think. After several rides where I brought just one water bottle, ran out, and had to beg other cyclists for water, I finally bought a CamelBak hydration system that has the capacity of four water bottles.

● Don't rely on your riding partners, or strangers on the trail, to supply you with water. They need the water they brought and it's not fair to drain them because you failed to bring enough.

● Don't expect to find a water source on your ride. Even on urban park rides, there won't always

🝗

DID YOU KNOW
Believe it or not, as recently as the 1980s, the International Olympic Committee prevented women access to certain sports because they believed, falsely, that sports training and competition could be detrimental to a woman's reproductive system.

be a working water fountain when you need one.

● Don't neglect to bring water on cold weather rides. Your body still needs to replace the large amounts of water it loses in dry, wintery air.

● Never drink from streams, lakes, or ponds unless you've treated or filtered the water first to kill bacteria.

● For hot rides, fill up your water bottle or hydration pack with some ice cubes or stick your partially filled water bottles in the freezer the night before. A cool drink on the trail is very refreshing.

Sports Drinks
I'm a big fan of water. On the trail, I drink from a CamelBak full of plain tap water (filtered through a Brita pitcher at home). But for long or strenuous rides in hot weather, I like to supplement my water with a bottle of flavored sports drink

containg carbohydrates and electrolytes. I've used Gatorade, All Sport, Powerade, and other, more expensive, mix-them-yourself performance drinks.

Sweet, fruity, slightly salty drinks like these hit the spot on the trail and encourage me to drink even more than I might have with just water, lessening my risk of dehydration. On my four-hour mountain bike rides, I feel I need the extra sugar, sodium, and minerals of a sports drink to replace those I've lost. (I could replace those substances just as well with a glass of milk and a banana, but they're more difficult to carry on the trail.)

If your rides are short (an hour or less) or not very strenuous, a sports drink isn't necessary.

NUTRITION 101
To stay healthy and energized for living and biking, you must consume carbohydrates, proteins, and fats. The *Physicians' Desk Reference Family Guide to Nutrition and Health* recommends eating a diet that consists of approximately 60 percent carbohydrates, 25 percent fat, and 15 percent protein. These three building blocks of nutrition contain vitamins, minerals, and fiber, which are also important for health. In addition, make sure your diet contains the iron, calcium, folic acid, and antioxidants (vitamins C and E and beta-carotene) women

Keep your body's fuel tank full by eating snacks (energy bars, trail mix, fruit, etc.) during your ride.

herself again.

An active person's diet should be built on a strong foundation of complex carbo-hydrates, which provide essen-tial fuel for energy throughout the work day and on a bike ride. Complex carbo-hydrates, or starches, like grains, pasta, vegetables, and pota-toes, provide excellent stored fuel when eaten prior to a ride and replenish the system when eaten afterward.

require. This isn't difficult if your diet includes plenty of dark green, yellow, and orange vegetables. Some low-fat or fat-free dairy products are also good sources of calcium.

Carbohydrates

Cyclists have a colorful name for that unpleasant feeling when their blood sugar level drops and they run out of fuel on a ride — the "bonk." The bonk manifests itself in different ways among different people. Some get lethargic, some get irritable, some get discombobulated. Mostly, though, they're just hungry. They need some carbs, fast. If you're riding with a friend who suddenly runs out of steam, starts complaining, and acts as if her whole world is crumbling, ask her to sit down and hand her an energy bar or a cookie. She'll thank you for it when she's feeling like

Simple carbohydrates, found in fruits and sugary foods, also give us energy and are effective for main-taining adequate blood sugar levels during exercise. Since I don't have much of a sweet tooth, I'm constantly amazed at how much I welcome a sugary snack on the trail. The same cloyingly sweet cookie or energy bar that I'd pass up for a snack at home really hits the spot after 10 miles of hard riding.

Proteins

The body does not store protein, which is necessary for healthy skin, organs, and muscle, the way it does carbohydrates. Therefore, protein

Fresh fruit is a great source of simple carbohydrates that help maintain blood sugar levels.

LONG TERM FITNESS: DON'T GIVE UP ON IT

It happens. You get excited about some new activity and buy expensive gear that sits in the basement most of the time. You feel guilty about the expense. You sell the equipment. You feel guilty about sitting around. You try a new activity.

But you can break this destructive cycle and stick with an activity that's fun and healthy.

● Find friends who mountain bike. (See Chapter 5 for tips on finding riding partners.) Try to find riding partners who'll push you to challenge yourself, and others who like to take it easy and ride for fun. (Sometimes it's the same person.)

● Plan an adventure. If you find yourself riding the same trails over and over, branch out. Ask at your bike shop or look in a local trail guide to find some longer, more remote and scenic trails in your area. In my hometown, I have several good trails to choose from. But just a few hours' drive away in the Mis-

must be eaten regularly. But, that doesn't mean you need to consume a lot of protein, even if you are athletic. Most Americans eat more than twice the amount of protein they need every day, and it is a myth that consuming more protein builds more or stronger muscles. On the contrary, there are some very good reasons for women, especially, to limit protein consumption to only what their bodies require. According to the *Harvard Women's Health Watch*, eating too much protein, especially animal protein, taxes the liver and kidneys. Studies also suggest that excess protein consumption causes the body to lose calcium, which can contribute to osteoporosis and bone fractures. In addition, many popular

DID YOU KNOW

A 1997 study published in the *New England Journal of Medicine* found that regular exercise dramatically decreases a woman's risk of breast cancer. A 20-year Norwegian study of 25,000 women revealed a 72 percent reduction in breast cancer risk for women who exercised regularly and were lean.

sources of protein (red meat, whole milk dairy products) are high in fat and cholesterol.

---

souri Ozarks, I can ride for miles through lush forests, sparkling creeks, and wide glades.

● Ride trails you like. Maybe that sounds obvious, but women sometimes try to please everyone but themselves. If your boyfriend or riding partners love that rocky trail with the killer climbs and you're up to it, by all means, ride it. But don't constantly suffer through trails you can't stand.

● Get a loved one involved. Take your sister, dad, or lover out on an easy trail some after-

noon. Pack a picnic lunch, take plenty of breaks, and enjoy the scenery. If you like each other's company and they're in decent shape, it might be a great time.

● Keep your bike clean and tuned. A mud-caked bike with squeaky brakes that shifts poorly is likely to keep you at home, sitting on the couch. Do what you have to to keep your bike clean, lubricated, and in good working order. Have a friend do it, take it to a bike shop, or better yet, learn to maintain it yourself.

Don't forget the sunscreen. There's evidence that the estrogen in women's bodies makes our skin more sensitive to sun damage than men's. Birth control pills, dermatological prescriptions, and some antibiotics can also make you burn faster.

A 125-pound woman requires about 45 grams of protein per day. Try to get more of your protein from plant sources like beans and whole grains and less from animal sources like meats, poultry, fish, and dairy products. When you do eat meat and dairy products, eat low-fat or fat-free.

Fats

If there's one word that occupies most women's minds at one point or another, it's this little one — fat. "I feel fat today." "Don't you have any low-fat salad dressing?" "She looks like she's getting fat." "I would never wear Lycra. I'm too fat."

Even a woman who has a fairly healthy body image finds the word "fat" creeping into her vocabulary more often than she'd like. Although

ENERGY BARS: WHO NEEDS 'EM?

Ah, energy bars. The luxury food of the well-heeled, recreational athlete. What would my mother say if she knew I spent two dollars on a tiny candy bar with added vitamins that claims to provide "Ultra Fuel for Extreme Efforts?" I shudder to think. I'm not that gullible. I know a plastic baggie full of fig bars or a PB & J on wheat bread is energy aplenty for

the word carries a lot of baggage in our vain society, we couldn't live without a little fat, since fats supply backup energy and maintain cellular functions in our bodies. We need the equivalent of about a tablespoon of oil every day.

Don't forget to apply sunscreen before you head out, and repeatedly during long rides.

Unfortunately, most Americans eat about eight times the amount of fat they need. We fry and mash our potatoes in it. We douse bowlfuls of healthy greens in it. We bake it into sweets, stir it into soups, and slather it on sandwiches. In addition to making us tubby, this excess fat contributes to a host of diseases, including heart disease and some cancers. While the mono- and polyunsaturated fats found in canola, olive, and soybean oil are better than the saturated fats found in meat, cheese, butter, and coconut oil, most of us would benefit from reducing our intake of all fats.

my needs. Same goes for bananas, pears, and raisins — high in carbs, inexpensive, easy to come by.

But for me, the advantage of an energy bar has nothing to do with all the advertising claims about essential vitamins, amino acids, and proteins. It's easy to get that from a balanced diet. I love them because of their convenience and indestructability. I can keep PowerBars around for months. Provided they're wrapped, I can fall on them, leave them in a hot car, dive in a lake with them, even drive a car over them. Rip open that foil-plastic covering and they're fine — 45 grams of fairly tasty get-up-and-go.

Try that with a fig bar or banana.

Pausing to drink water and have a snack also gives you a chance to enjoy your riding partners and your surroundings.

I find the connection between food and health interesting, and, as a result, I read all kinds of information about nutrition, from pamphlets in doctors' offices to medical journal articles, to bestselling diet books. If there's one dietary rule of thumb most Americans should follow, it's to eat more carbohydrates, less fat, and less protein. Based on current scientific opinion regarding good nutrition and my own experiences with food, I try to eat a diet

EATING FOR HEALTH, PERFORMANCE, AND WEIGHT-CONTROL

I'm not a licensed dietician, but I am something of an amateur nutritionist.

PLAN AHEAD FOR HEALTHY EATING

Eating healthfully can be difficult during hectic times. When deadlines, appointments, and family responsibilities leave me pressed for time, I occasionally succumb to the fast-food drive-through and junk-food vending machine for sustenance and comfort. To prevent these indulgences in Quarter Pounders with Cheese and Snickers bars, I try to anticipate busy times.

On an evening prior to an upcoming "Hell Week," I take some time to shop for ingredients to make healthy bag lunches (pasta salad, baby carrots, fruit Newtons, fat-free yogurt) and quick-fix dinners (spaghetti

The author's favorite low-calorie, high-energy breakfast: oatmeal topped with fresh fruit.

rich in fresh fruits, vegetables, beans, and whole grains, and low in high-fat meat and dairy products.

During the winter of 1998, determined to lose the last five pounds that even regular, vigorous exercise and a "balanced" diet wouldn't budge, I eliminated meat and high-fat dairy products from my diet. I ate lots of beans and rice, pasta with vegetables, veggie pizza, and oriental stir-fries with tofu. My

with marinara sauce, black bean and veggie burritos). I know if I come home after work and all I have in the fridge is eggs and cheese, I'll fix a high-fat omelette; if I have some veggies and rice on hand, I can enjoy a healthy stir-fry.

Running out of ideas for good, quick meals? Check your library or bookstore's cookbook section. There are literally hundreds of great low-fat and vegetarian cookbooks out now, many of them geared to the cook who's in a hurry. A few of my favorites are *Short-Cut Vegetarian*, by Lorna Sass; *The Compassionate Cook*, by Ingrid Newkirk; and *The New Moosewood Cookbook* by Mollie Katzen.

JEN'S TOP TEN TRAIL SNACKS

- Chocolate Almond Clif Bar
- Carrot Cake Clif Bar
- Cheese sandwich and apple
- Almond butter and apricot jelly sandwich
- Peanut butter and strawberry jelly sandwich
- Peanut butter and banana sandwich
- Raspberry Newtons
- Fig Newtons
- Nature Valley Granola Bar (Oats and Honey)
- Quaker Oatmeal Squares and raisins

favorite breakfast was oatmeal cooked in soy milk, topped with sliced fruit or raisins. For snacks, I'd blend up frozen fruit and skim milk smoothies. I'd buy myself a special, healthy treat now and then — a jar of gourmet salsa, exotically flavored carbonated water, a pint of expensive, but tasty out-of-season berries — to keep things interesting. I ate heartily, but healthfully.

Those five pounds disappeared quickly and I felt great; not weighed down and bloated from fatty, salty foods. And I felt good knowing this way of eating would help protect my health in the long run, as diets high in plant foods and low in high-fat animal foods are linked to lower incidence of diseases such as heart disease, certain cancers, adult-onset diabetes, stroke, osteoporosis, hypertension, and obesity.

The immediate benefit? When climbing a hill on my bike, my breakfast of oatmeal and fruit gives me energy and lightness I never felt after eating an egg, ham, and cheese sandwich. Another believer in a low-fat diet — racer Michele Kean — says she frequently hears other racers bemoaning their poor performance on the trail after eating heavy, greasy meals.

"They eat chicken-fried steak and scrambled eggs and then complain about their performance, yet they refuse to believe their diet has anything to do with it. Of course it does," she says. "But I just smile and shake my head. Good eating is my ace in the hole."

Stephanie Ashley began to think about food differently and lost 30 pounds after getting into mountain biking.

"Before, I really didn't think about food at all. I just ate whatever I wanted based on my mood. Now I consciously try to pick healthier foods, instead of going solely on my whims. I feel much better. And riding up hills is easier without those 30 pounds."

URBAN
RIDING
AND
COMMUTING

Why discuss urban riding and bike commuting in a book about mountain biking? Many reasons.

Most of us don't live at a mountain resort where we can leave our cabin every morning and spend the day riding backwoods single-track. Most of us have jobs that require us to live in cities, suburbs, and towns. And statistics show that many women rarely venture off-road with their mountain bikes, preferring instead to ride them around town.

Additionally, the two types of riding complement each other. Riding your bike regularly in town during the week — to work, to the store, to the movies — keeps your muscles and cardiovascular system in shape for vigorous weekend trail rides. Off-road riding hones bike-handling skills that are essential for dodging potholes, keeping your balance at intersections, making quick stops, and hopping curbs. The more you ride, the better you'll get at both types of riding.

I have learned through experience that a mountain bike is a superb vehicle for transportation, offering a fun, healthy, money-saving, non-polluting means of getting from place to place.

Stay alert and wear brightly-colored clothing when riding in traffic.

WHY A MOUNTAIN BIKE?

In my opinion, a modified mountain bike is the best bike available for urban riding. Its fat tires absorb shock better than skinny ones, making for a more comfortable ride

ASK THE EXPERT
DEB RIDGWAY,
URBAN CYCLIST, St. Louis, Missouri

Deb Ridgway, is a graduate student and bike advocate who rides her bike five miles to work and school four days a week. She also rides her bike to the movies, to street festivals, to the grocery store, and on recreational rides with friends.

Q: Why did you begin using your bike for transportation?

A: When I started grad school I didn't have a car and had to rely on public transportation. Later, I realized that I wasn't too far from work to easily ride the distance on my bike. At first, riding in traffic was scary, and it still is sometimes. But I take it seriously: I abide by the rules of the road and learn tips from friends. The more I do it, the more confident I become.

Q: What do you like about bike commuting?

A: It's a great opportunity to fit exercise into my schedule. I enjoy the personal time, riding through the park on my way to and from work. I experience things — the fresh morning air, the flowers in

(fatter tires are not as prone to punctures and less likely to get stuck in road ruts, storm sewer grates, and bridge expansion joints). Its durable wheels and components stand up better to potholes, and the upright riding (and shifting) position lets you anticipate hazards and respond quickly. And its beefy frame can transport a load with ease.

Now, what do I mean by *modified*? While a regular mountain bike works fine, several alterations — smooth tires, tire liners, fenders, rack, panniers, mirror, lighting system, and lock — can make a mountain bike even better for riding in town. Each of these accessories is discussed in Chapter 2.

A mountain bike equipped with a huge mud flap for winter commuting in Minneapolis, Minnesota.

---

the park — that I can't from a car or the bus. And since I drive my car only once a week during the summer, it saves me quite a bit on gas, maintenance, and insurance.

Q: How do you deal with occasional harassment from motorists?
A: If I get the chance, I try to tell them as nicely as possible that the law says I have a right to be there and that they need to respect me and share the road. I have to watch my temper, because I have yelled and cursed in the past, but that's dangerous and doesn't accomplish anything.

Q: What advice do you have for women new to bike commuting?
A: Don't be afraid to try. It's easy to make tons of excuses for why you can't do it, but most of them are solvable. The first time you ride to work, try it on your day off when you have plenty of time. Ask a friend who's a cyclist to help you find a good route and ride it with you. Educate yourself and be prepared. Carry a spare tube, tire levers, and pump and know how to use them to fix a flat. Once you're comfortable with the routine, you'll be amazed how much you'll enjoy it.

DID YOU KNOW

According to surveys by *Bicycling* magazine, the number of people who bike to work has grown more than 20 percent in the last five years to approximately seven million.

If you ride your mountain bike both off and on the road, an extra set of wheels fitted with slick tires is a worthwhile investment that will keep you from constantly changing from slick to knobby tires. If you find that you can spin wildly on pavement even when in your highest (hardest) gears, and you use your mountain bike primarily for in-town riding, consider having your bike's low gearing altered to better accommodate pavement riding.

KEEPING CLEAN, DEALING WITH CLOTHES AND HAIR
The Shower Dilemma

Many companies provide showers, lockers, or other bike-friendly facilities at the workplace. However, some people think that if there's no shower there, they can't ride to work. Don't let this excuse keep you from riding. Washing up at the sink, applying talcum powder and deodorant, and putting on clean, dry clothes works very well to keep you fresh. If you have nowhere private to wash up at work, use disposable wipes or moist towelettes to clean up

ASK THE EXPERT
MARY WOOD,
URBAN CYCLIST, St. Louis, Missouri

Mary Wood, is a computer network administrator who four years ago sold her car and began using her bike as her primary form of transportation.

Q: Why did you decide to give up your car and use your bike instead?

A: At that time, I was working a full-time and a part-time job to cover my bills and I felt overwhelmed by working all the time. In order to quit my part-time job, I did some brainstorming about how I could cut my expenses radically and I kept coming back to my car. It was my second biggest expense at $400 a month. I thought I'd get rid of the car for a year, pay off some bills, and buy a cheap car at the end of the year. But I learned that by using my bike, I could get around easily and continue saving about $4000 a year.

in a restroom. Or look for a health club near work. Some clubs will provide bike commuter services like secure bike storage, showers, lockers, and changing facilities at reasonable rates. It never hurts to ask.

With the right waterproof clothing and storage and the right attitude, even rain need not stop you from commuting to work.

Clothing Tips

Do you ride around town wearing pants or jeans, rather than shorts? Try wearing dark-colored or black ones so they won't show grease stains if you happen to bump your chain. To keep pants from getting caught in the chain, which can be very dangerous, use an ankle strap made of reflective nylon webbing and Velcro.

Q: What reactions did you get from co-workers when you gave up your car in favor of a bike?
A: A few people expressed anger toward me. My supervisor voiced concerns that it would affect my attendance (it didn't). But I think it just didn't fit into the corporate image. Luckily, the company I now work for has no problem with a woman riding her bike to work.
Q: What misconceptions have you overcome using your bike to get around?

A: So many people think, "If my car ever gives up the ghost, I'm doomed." I've learned that's simply not true. We've just lost our resourcefulness. I have a full array of backpacks and panniers that make errands and grocery shopping painless. When I really need a ride somewhere, I buy lunch for a friend in exchange for a lift, or I take a cab or a bus. If I want to take a road trip or if out-of-town visitors are coming, I rent a car for a few days.

The author, fully out-fitted for her daily commute.

If you bike in skirts, avoid long, flowing ones unless you have a chain guard. Shorter, flared skirts are better, and "skorts" or split skirts are best. Clothing manufacturer Zoic makes a cute, functional skort designed especially for cycling with a CoolMax liner short underneath a Cordura/Lycra skirt. GKA Wear also makes bike skorts. (See "Sources & Resources.") The combination of my comfortable padded shorts topped with a short, flared skirt is perfect for those times when I want to pop in and out of shops without getting funny looks.

MYTHS ABOUT URBAN RIDING

MYTH: Riding in traffic is much too dangerous. Drivers are out to kill cyclists.
FACT: Most drivers are safe, courteous, and law-abiding. A cyclist who is visible, alert, and knows how to ride effectively in traffic is safer than you'd think.
MYTH: It's safer to ride facing oncoming traffic so a car can't hit you from behind.
FACT: Neophyte cyclists commonly fear being hit from behind by a car while riding in traffic, but only a tiny percentage of bike accidents actually happen this way. Statistically, riding against traffic is the more dangerous way to ride. It's much safer to ride with the flow of traffic.
MYTH: I can't ride because there's no sidewalk or bike path.
FACT: Although it may seem illogical, accident statistics show that cycling on the roadway may actually be safer than using urban bike paths and sidewalks. Studies have found that the accident rate for cycling on paths separate from the road is 2.6 times higher than that of cycling on the road. The higher accident rate for bikepaths can be attributed in part to bike-car conflicts at intersections and cross streets, and collisions with pedestrians or other bikes on the path.

Finding a place to hang sweaty bike clothes to dry out for the ride home can be a challenge. If your bike is stored in a place where no one will bother it, you can drape your clothes over the top tube and handlebars. Many office coat closets are unused during warm weather and may be available (you might want to stick an air freshener in too). Plastic adhesive hooks are inexpensive and easily stuck in unobtrusive places — behind your office door, on the side of a bookcase, in a little-used supply closet, under your desk — and provide a good place to hang clothes.

Helmet and Hair Issues

Most helmets have removable foam pads to absorb sweat and make the helmet fit snugly. If your helmet's getting smelly, remove the pads, wash them in warm, soapy water, let them air dry, and reattach them inside the helmet. Cleaning the pads periodically will keep your hair smelling fresh after a ride. Bike shops and helmet manufacturers sell replacement foam pads if yours wear out before your helmet does. The dreaded helmet-hair look can be avoided if you: (1) wear your hair short; (2) pull your hair into a pony-tail, French braid, or up-do after riding; (3) keep a blow dryer, curling iron, or hair styling products at work; (4) are satisfied with the natural look of combed, but not styled, hair.

If your hair tends to whip around or fall into your eyes, be sure to pull

it back securely before you ride. One unfortunate experience taught me to keep barrettes and hair bands with me at all times. In the midst of climbing the biggest hill on my ride to work, a lock of hair fell over my face, obscuring my vision. I used one hand to brush it away, and learned instantly that standing to climb requires two hands on the handle-bars. The worst part was that as I fell to the pavement, my boss — a competitive road biker whom I greatly admire — happened to be driving by and saw the whole thing. I was fine, but my pride was injured.

MY RIDE TO WORK

6:00 A.M. I awaken early to the rude buzz of my alarm clock. This is the hard part: getting up 40 minutes earlier to ride to work. Once I'm up and in the shower, however, I'm looking forward to starting the day with a

?

DID YOU KNOW
Increasingly, metropolitan transit authorities are making buses, trains, and subways accessible to bikes. Check with your local transit system for details on how to take your bike on board to shorten your trip.

The author brings her bike aboard her commuter train for a 15-minute ride that makes her 15-mile commute feasible.

ride. Why shower *before* riding? Since there's no shower at my office, I stay cleaner if I shower at home first and sponge off at the sink at work after my ride.

6:15 A.M. A breakfast of hot oatmeal and fruit in the winter and cold cereal or a bagel in the summer gives me the energy I need for my ride. If I ride on an empty stomach, I feel terrible once I get to work. If I'm running late, I'll bring an energy bar and an apple to eat on the train.

6:45 A.M. I pull on a pair of padded bike shorts (with casual shorts over the top) and a T-shirt. I feel more comfortable and less conspicuous — especially during my 20-minute train ride — if I'm wearing normal clothing rather than form-fitting bike clothes.

7:00 A.M. Since I packed lunch, work clothes, and toiletries into my backpack the night before, all that remains is to make sure I have train fare and adequately inflated tires before I head out the door.

7:05 A.M. Traffic at this time of the morning is surprisingly light in the working-class residential and warehousing district of the city that I ride through. After more than a year of riding the same route, I know exactly which potholes to avoid and which ones I can handle on my front suspension mountain bike. I glance behind for a break in traffic, then signal a left turn to merge into the middle lane.

7:30 A.M. Arriving at the train station, I realize how lucky I am to be able to bring my bike aboard the commuter train and relax for a leisurely, air-conditioned 15 minutes.

My home is 15 miles from work, and without the train to shorten my ride, I'd rarely pedal the distance. I board

TIPS FOR RIDING SAFELY IN TRAFFIC

● Ride with traffic, not against it.
● Obey traffic laws, signs, and stoplights.
● Use hand signals when changing lanes or turning.
● Avoid riding on sidewalks. Motorists exiting driveways and cross streets don't expect a cyclist on the sidewalk and may hit you.
● Stay to the right, but don't hug the curb. A slight mistake when you're riding too far to the right could cause you to lose control and take a spill. Also, road edges tend to collect glass, leaves and other detritus and can be dangerously full of potholes.
● Ride predictably. Don't swerve in and out between parked cars.
● Don't get "doored." When riding alongside parked cars, look in each car as you approach to see if anyone's inside. Allow yourself plenty of room in case a driver or passenger opens a door. Take the traffic lane if you have to.
● Watch for the cut-off! Oncoming drivers may attempt to turn left in front of you, even though you have the right of way.

Overtaking drivers may attempt to pass, then swerve in front of you to make a sudden right turn.
● Be visible. Even on sunny days, you're more likely to be seen if you're wearing bright colors like yellow, orange, hot pink, red, or anything fluorescent. At night and during low-light conditions, make sure both you and your bike are well lighted and have plenty of reflective material. It is not enough to be seen from only the front and rear. Jackets, vests, and pants made from new fabrics like Illuminite contain reflective materials so that your whole body, not just your pedals and handlebars, reflect the light of vehicle headlights.
● Learn from the experts. The League of American Bicyclists offers "Effective Cycling" classes around the country that teach valuable on-road cycling skills. And Dave Glowacz, an Effective Cycling instructor and a city cyclist for 30 years, has compiled a book of valuable suggestions and information called, *Urban Bikers' Tricks and Tips: Low-Tech and No-Tech Ways to Find, Ride, and Keep a Bicycle.* See "Sources & Resources."

Obeying traffic laws and signs and using hand signals are essential to safe riding in traffic.

the last car and stand with my bike in a vestibule at the rear.

7:50 A.M. Pedaling again, this time on a frontage road in a suburb, I can see that vehicle traffic on the interstate has backed up as a result of construction a few miles ahead. I'd be idling in that traffic too, if I weren't on my bike.

8:15 A.M. I arrive at work with 15 minutes to spare, say good morning to another bike-commuting co-worker, roll my bike into a storage room, and head to the restroom to clean up. My routine of washing off, sprinkling baby powder on my damp skin, applying deodorant, getting into clean clothes, brushing my hair, and applying makeup takes about 10 minutes. I use the remaining five minutes to hang my bike clothes up to dry and get a cup of coffee. Although my ride totals only five miles, I feel energized and wide awake.

I ride to work for many reasons: to stay in shape, to prevent wear and tear on my car, to set an example for others, to avoid polluting the air. But most of all, I ride because biking makes me *feel* more. Sometimes the sights, sounds, and smells are beautiful — crickets, cicadas, and honeysuckle. Sometimes they are appalling — acrid car exhaust, children running barefoot through vacant, glass–littered lots. But biking to work gives me a chance to know my city intimately. Driving only numbs me.

MAKE THE
MOST OF
YOUR RIDE

In a perfect world, one could head out anytime to enjoy an invigorating, stress-relieving bike ride without a care. But a positive attitude alone is not enough to ensure a hassle-free ride. It's best to be aware of the things that could affect your ride — harassment, an animal encounter, a sore behind — and know how to deal with them.

SAFETY
Reporting Harassment

If someone harasses or attacks you, report the incident to authorities — police, land managers, and on-site security personnel. Make sure your complaint is documented so law enforcement officials can follow through.

On the road, it's never smart to confront bad or abusive drivers. Some are looking for a fight wherever they can find one; others feel so invincible inside their steel shells that they might be dangerous. Even the driver who unintentionally cuts you off is liable to get a bad attitude about cyclists if he gets cursed at. If you choose to confront a driver about a bonehead traffic move, keep your cool. Don't yell. Don't get personal. Calmly explain how his actions endangered your safety. If he questions, explain that you have a right to

♀

WOMAN-TO-WOMAN

RIDING ALONE SAFELY

"Mountain biking alone at my favorite trail once, I rounded a bend to come face to face with two guys on motorcycles. It made me mad, partly because they startled me and also because motorcycles aren't allowed on the trail. Flustered, I blurted out, 'You can't ride here,' and as soon as I did I regretted it since I was so vulnerable out there. I spent the rest of my ride looking over my shoulder and listening for their motors. Nothing bad happened, but it really made me think about my safety."

Stephanie Ashley, art teacher,
Hillsboro, Missouri

be on the road. Some cyclists carry a copy of their state's statutes regarding bicycles to show unenlightened motorists.

License plate numbers can be very helpful for prosecuting or reprimanding dangerous drivers. If you have a valid complaint against a motorist, try to get his or her license plate number to help police locate the driver (carry a pen and small notebook to write it down). If the driver is operating a truck, delivery vehicle, or taxi cab, complain to his or her company dispatcher. In some states, the department of motor vehicles will give you the name and insurance carrier of the person to whom a license plate number is registered so you can send their insurer a warning letter. Check with your state or local bike advocacy

organization. Some groups will send a warning letter to the offender. The Texas Bicycle Coalition, for example, is assembling a database of bad drivers, and plans to have attorneys telephone the offenders to warn them of the penalties for threatening cyclists.

Protect Yourself From Attacks

Cycling safety expert Dave Glowacz does not recommend the use of pepper sprays, knives, or handguns for personal protection because of the likelihood that they will be used against the victim they were meant to protect. For example, to use pepper spray effectively, an attacker must be downwind of you or you risk getting the stuff in your eyes, nose, and mouth. But since most attacks are unexpected, you likely won't have time to think about which way the wind is blowing. Also, most weapons are inaccessible in a surprise attack (unless you ride with your hand on your gun). If you plan to carry pepper spray or a weapon, take some time to learn how to use it properly. Glowacz is a bigger fan of women's self-defense classes than weapons. He also recommends loud noisemakers, like whistles and air horns, to scare off bad guys. And always tell someone where you are going and when you will return.

Play it Safe With Animals

DOGS Talk to any long-time cyclist and she'll probably have a dog story for you. On my ride to work, I look forward to racing past a feisty border collie in the fenced yard of a quiet subdivision. I think he looks forward to it too. His herding instinct causes him to race alongside me for the length of his fence, barking the entire time. It must be the most exciting event of his day.

Bison encounter, Antelope Island, Great Salt Lake, northern Utah.

But fenced-in, suburban dogs aren't your concern, I'm sure. You, like me, are more worried about big, snarling Rottweilers that run free on rural gravel roads. I can tell you that kind of dog story too. Mine ended with me shouting, "NO! GO HOME!" in the most authoritative voice I could muster. It worked.

If a dog seems threatening, you can always ride fast, but don't count on being able to outrun him. If you can ride one-handed, squirt a pursuing dog in the face with your water bottle (Gatorade or other acidic citrus drinks work especially well). Lower your voice. When shouting a com-

mand at a threatening dog, a loud, low, masculine-sounding pitch works better than a feminine, high-pitched voice. If a dog has you cornered, one unusual tip that Dave Glowacz insists works surprisingly well is to shout, "COME HERE!" in a "master's really mad at pooch" voice. The dog pursuing Glowacz backed down, turned tail, and ran for home. If you're off your bike, try to keep the bike between you and the dog so you can use it as a shield. If a dog attacks you, defend yourself. Kick, punch, or stab — hard! Report dog attacks to police and remember what a dog looks like and, if possible, which house it came from. If you can identify a dog and locate its owner to verify that the dog's not rabid, you can avoid a series of painful rabies shots.

HORSES AND PACK ANIMALS Horses are easily spooked and many are deathly afraid of bikes. (You might be afraid too if some Lycra-clad weirdo snuck up on you in the woods.) Never startle a horse or other pack animal. It might throw its rider or kick someone nearby (like you). If you see an equestrian approaching,

FIRST AID IN THE WILDS

Video footage of mountain bikers careening down hills at 60 mph may have your friends and family oohing and ahhing about how extreme and dangerous the sport is, but most real bikers know the truth: It's only as scary as you make it. While a few cuts and bruises are to be expected, none of my mountain biker girlfriends has ever been seriously injured on the trail. It's smart to carry a small first aid kit, however, for those times when your bike goes one way and you go the other. More tips:

● If you frequent backcountry trails that are miles from medical assistance, invest in a wilderness first-aid manual or course.

● Trailhead information boards sometimes post the name, phone number, and location of the nearest hospital. It pays to know in advance where they are or have a good road map of the area in case of an emergency.

● Don't use creek or lake water to rinse cuts and scrapes. Instead, use a squirt from your water bottle or carry a few baby wipes.

● Tired of ugly bruises on your legs? I've had good luck with the homeopathic remedy Arnica montana, which has prevented discoloring bruises from forming even after a big bang against a rock. As a beginner, I carried a small vial in my bike bag. It is most effective if taken before the skin begins to discolor. Applying ice and elevating the affected body part also helps.

● Cellular phones can provide instant communication in emergencies, but they are easily broken on rough single-track, and many trails are outside cell range. Also, cellular phones tend to give backcountry visitors a false sense of security, as if simply possessing one somehow minimizes danger. If you carry a phone, protect it in a padded case and make sure the battery is charged. And don't even think about calling in the search-and-rescue team unless you're in a dire situation.

slow down, announce your presence, dismount your bike, and stand to the side of the trail. If the horse is still reluctant to pass, lay your bike down on the ground. Talking quietly helps the horse identify you as a human.

WILD ANIMALS Some of my coolest encounters with animals in the wild have come while on a mountain bike. I've silently come upon wild turkey, deer, foxes, and owls. But in parts of the country

Moving a turtle to safety along a trail in the Meramec River bottoms, eastern Missouri.

where mountain lions and bears are common, it's prudent to make noise to warn wild animals of your presence. This prevents you from surprising a large predator who might think you're a deer bolting down the trail. A friend of mine who rides in the grizzly-bear territory of British Columbia always ties jingle bells to her handlebars. If she's feeling espe-

cially vulnerable, she'll sing loudly as she rides. There also seems to be safety in numbers. Bears aren't known to attack parties of more than four people.

SNAKES Despite people's fear of anything slithery, most snakes are harmless and very interesting to look at. Read through a snake identification guide (preferably with full-color

Photo opportunity on Going-to-the-Sun Road in Glacier National Park, Montana. The sudden appearance of a biker can startle animals more than hikers approaching on foot.

photos) to learn more about the snakes that live where you ride. You'll be able to better tell venomous snakes from non-venomous ones, where they're likely to be found, and other facts about these fascinating creatures. Be cautious in the following situations: carrying your bike over big logs, crossing creeks or flooded areas, passing through rocky areas and glades, and riding at night, when snakes are most active.

If you are bitten, try to stay calm. Becoming hysterical will only make the effects of a snakebite worse. Take some comfort in the fact that a fairly large percentage of the time (25–40 percent), snakes inject no venom when they bite, sparing you a lot of pain and swelling. Get medical assistance as soon as possible. Before

swelling begins, remove anything constricting from the affected limb — rings, bracelets, watches. Do not attempt any of the "cut and suck" or tourniquet snakebite remedies. They can do more harm than good if administered by an amateur. Some doctors recommend a device called the Extractor. It uses suction to remove up to a third of the injected venom if used soon after a snakebite. If possible, lie quietly while someone goes for help. But if you're miles from nowhere, riding or walking out will get you the help you need faster than being carried or waiting for a rescue. The treatment for a venomous snakebite is antivenin, which must be given under medical supervision because of the possibility of allergic reaction. If you ride in an area with many poisonous snakes, ask your doctor to prescribe an antivenin that you can carry into the backcountry.

Hitting the Trails During Hunting Season

Most guidebooks say, "DON'T!" and that's good, safe advice. But since hunting seasons tend to fall in the middle of the best riding times (spring or fall), some of us like to put on the orange, tie some bells on the handlebars, and head out anyway. Depending on where you live, hunting seasons can last from one to four weeks. Ask conservation or wildlife officials when the local hunting seasons begin and end, and which trails tend to get overrun with hunters. During hunting season, forest roads are safer than deep woods single-track. Or you could stick to state and county parks and other areas where hunting is prohibited. Wear extremely bright colors (so-called hunter's orange is best) and avoid anything white. I retired my white bike helmet early after realizing it might resemble a whitetailed deer's rear end scampering through the woods.

COMFORT ISSUES

Saddle Soreness 101: For Women Only

Dr. Jeffrey Baker, a cycling enthusiast and family physician in State College, Pennsylvania, has made treating cyclists' saddle soreness somewhat of a specialty. He regularly

If you hit the trail during deer-hunting season, wear extremely bright colors and avoid white.

consults with cyclists and has published articles on the subject in bike magazines. Solving the posterior problems that conspire to keep women off bikes is usually a matter of understanding our bodies, practicing good hygiene, and using common sense, he says. In addition to getting a saddle that fits properly, covered in Chapter 2, he suggests the following:

● Proper bike fit. Correct seat height, fore/aft, and reach are all factors in to making your ride comfortable. Notice how hunched over or upright you sit on your bike; too upright and you'll put pressure on your butt, too bent over and your genitals will feel the effects.

● If you experience chafing or

genital soreness while riding, try working a lubricant into your short's chamois. Bag Balm, Assos' chamois cream, Chamois Butt'r, and good old Vaseline all work.

Shaving in the genital region can cause irritation. It exposes new skin to a potentially troublesome situation by removing protective layers of skin cells.

Beware of wet shorts. They can stick to your skin and chafe, and they provide the warm, moist environment that bacterial and fungal microbes prefer. Riding in the rain and using your bike shorts as an impromptu swim suit can sometimes cause problems.

Keep your bottom meticulously clean and never wear dirty bike shorts. Women's bodies are designed in such a way that bacteria don't have far to travel to get into the vagina or urethra, where they can cause vaginitis or a urinary tract infection. Riding in sweaty, unwashed shorts further increases the risk of infection.

If you have painful, pimple-like bumps on your rump, they could be saddle sores. These boils form when a hair follicle becomes inflamed and infected as a result of friction and doesn't receive sufficient oxygen, or time away from the bike seat, to heal. Treat saddle sores by cleansing the

TIPS FOR AVOIDING NUMB HANDS AND WRISTS

Wear padded gloves. They help absorb shock, and prevent blistered palms, and protect your hands if you fall.

Don't lock your elbows. Keep a firm grip, not a stranglehold on the handlebars and bend your arms slightly to allow them to take up the bumps.

Install bar ends on your handlebars for a different hand position, or a suspension fork to absorb more wrist-rattling shock.

Take breaks to rotate your wrists, wiggle your fingers, and give your hands a rest.

Some doctors recommend taking B-complex vitamin supplements and anti-inflammatory medications to reduce pain and numbness in the hands.

If your job requires a repetitive hand motion, like typing, you may be more likely to experience hand and wrist pain on the bike. Take extra precautions to prevent soreness and injury.

If your wrist pain or hand numbness doesn't dissipate, see your doctor. You may require treatment.

area, lancing the boil with a sterile needle, and letting it drain, applying an antibacterial ointment, and staying off the bike until it heals. Allowing the wound to breathe will speed the healing. An oral antibiotic like erythromycin or tetracycline helps prevent reinfection.

● Tender tush? If you haven't been on a bike for a while, you probably just need to ride more to toughen up your rear end. For years, I have jokingly referred to this as "building up the butt callus," but it's a real phenomenon, according to Dr. Baker. The more you ride, the tougher, firmer, and thicker the skin and supportive tissues under your ischial tuberosities, or sit bones, get.

● Can sex and hard mountain biking go hand in hand? That depends on the individual. Sex before or after a long, vigorous ride can cause further irritation, or not cause any problems at all.

Neck and Shoulder Pain

Stiff, aching necks or shoulders are common among beginning mountain bikers and intermediate or advanced bikers who take long rides. Straining and scrunching these muscles constantly while riding can cause them to tighten. The most effective way to prevent this is to ride a bike that fits. Do you feel too stretched out when holding onto the handlebars? Your bike's top tube or stem may be too long. Refer to the section on bike fit in Chapter 1 for suggestions on

altering an improperly fitting bike.

Some gentle neck rolls and shoulder stretches before, during and after a ride help relax tight muscles. On the bike, try to remember to keep your shoulders relaxed. After a long ride, a luxurious soak in a hot bath soothes tired, tense muscles. And if you're lucky enough to know a good masseuse, take advantage.

Knee Pain

Most cyclists experience some knee pain at one time or another. Getting nearly a full leg extension during your pedal stroke can lessen your chances of having knee pain. So can wearing knee pads, since riding with a banged-up knee can increase your pain and further irritate a stress or overuse injury. Treat your knees right; they're hard to replace. Keep knees covered when riding in temperatures below 60 degrees. Don't ride in too high a gear. Pedaling in a lower gear allows you to spin easily and avoid stressing the knees. And stretch gently before and after riding.

Back Pain

Like many other body aches, back pain while cycling can arise from a poorly fitting bike. Have your position on the bike checked at a good bike shop. Besides an existing injury, the other common cause of low back pain is weak abdominal muscles. The solution? Abdominal crunches. To reduce lower back pain (and that little kangaroo pouch) try to do 100 to 150 crunches (bent knee sit-ups) every day.

Effects of Altitude

Scenario: You're taking a bike trip to Crested Butte, Colorado, your one big vacation of the year. You've put in many bike miles on local Midwestern trails in preparation, and feel strong. But after only four miles of riding in the mountains the first day, you're exhausted. You head back to the lodge with a headache, feeling short of breath and nauseous.

Altitude affects people differently. Usually, even flatlanders can travel from sea level to 7000 or 8000 feet with minimal effects. However, when you begin to exceed that altitude, your body's systems compensate for the reduced amount of oxygen. Mild altitude sickness can result in headache, nausea, dizziness, loss of appetite, fatigue, and shortness of breath.

To adapt to the thinner air at high altitudes and avoid feeling sick, take your time. People who live at sea level are especially vulnerable to higher elevations for the first few days of a trip. Try to schedule an easy sightseeing or relaxation day when you first arrive in the mountains. Don't plan long, vigorous rides until you've been at that altitude for

PREVENTING AND TREATING KNEE PAIN

⬤ Have a reputable bike mechanic check your position on the bike, including saddle height and fore/aft, and if you use clipless pedals, have him or her position your shoe cleats correctly. Pedals/cleats should have "float," or movement that allows for a natural foot position on the pedal, but no more than five or six degrees' worth.

⬤ Keep anti-inflammatory pain relievers, like Advil, Motrin, or generic ibuprofen, in your bike bag and take the recommended dosage if you fall and bang your knee.

⬤ Ice the location where you feel pain or see swelling. Keep a bag of frozen corn or peas in your freezer at home for this purpose. A small cooler with ice and cold drinks in your car at the trailhead can both refresh you and soothe a sore knee after a ride.

⬤ Don't overtrain. Take some time away from riding if you're in pain.

⬤ If your knee pain is severe or recurring, see a doctor, physical therapist, or chiropractic sports physician who can diagnose and treat the problem through rehabilitative exercise and other methods.

Cycling high in Colorado's San Juan Range. To avoid the effects of high altitude, take time to adjust before heading out on long rides or ones that gain lots of elevation.

a couple of days. Drink lots of water and avoid alcohol, which can lead to dehydration. A mild altitude headache can be treated with aspirin, ibuprofen, or Tylenol. But the only real cure for altitude sickness is to descend. Usually 500 to 1000 feet does the trick.

If you or a companion begin to suffer from slurred speech, poor coordination, or fuzzy thinking at high altitudes, go downhill as soon as possible. These symptoms indicate advanced altitude sickness and, if ignored, could lead to cerebral or pulmonary edema (blood plasma in the brain or lungs) and death. In the United States, the average elevation at which an edema occurs is only 12,000 feet.

Poison Ivy, Oak, and Sumac

More than anything else — bruises, heat, physical exhaustion, or ticks — poison ivy very nearly scared me off mountain biking as a beginner. Several days after a ride, I'd start itching like mad, watch as patches of little liquid-filled blisters appeared on my legs, and wait impatiently until they disappeared a week or two later. I became an expert on poison ivy. I learned that the degree of sensitivity to the "poison" plants varies from person to person. Fair-skinned people and children seem to be more susceptible than others. I found, through experience, that the offending oils of poison ivy, oak, and sumac can be transported by pets, bikes, clothing, shoes, and camping equipment. Any news report, magazine article, or pharmacist's advice I encountered on the subject was carefully noted on my ever-lengthening list of preventatives or remedies to try.

Then one day I all but stopped getting poison ivy. I've been exposed to it dozens of times in the last few years, but I just don't react to it as severely as I used to. In *The Poison Ivy, Oak, & Sumac Book,* author Thomas Anderson notes that some people seem to develop a resistance upon repeated exposure, but no conclusive evidence of such a tolerance exists. Scientists do know that as the immune system weakens with age, the body can become less sensitive to allergens like the urushiol oil of the "poison plants." Whatever the reason, I'm thankful for the respite.

AVOIDING THE PERILS OF POISON IVY, OAK, AND SUMAC

● Keep skin that may contact plants covered. If you're susceptible, wear tights or leggings when you're in the woods to protect your legs from the plants' urushiol oil.

● Contrary to popular belief, the fluid in skin eruptions cannot make a rash spread. Breakage of the tiny blisters, however, makes infection more likely. Keep open blisters clean and use an antiseptic.

● Over-the-counter antihistamines like Benadryl may alleviate some of the itching that accompanies a poison ivy, oak, or sumac rash.

● Topical steriods like hydrocortisone may temporarily relieve itching and burning, but should not be used for more than a week and never on the face or genitals.

● Many over-the-counter remedies like calamine lotion, Ivarest, and Ivy Dry contain an astringent that may help reduce oozing and inflammation and promote healing.

Between 75 and 85 percent of all humans are potentially allergic to urushiol. In some extremely sensitive people, the plants can cause severe dermatitis, swelling, and/or breathing problems. These people should seek treatment from a physician. Most of us simply react to the poison plants by developing an itching, burning rash. Preventing contact with poison ivy, oak, and sumac by learning to identify them is smart, but tricky because of their various forms. Once afflicted with the rash, I've found minimal relief in the creams, salves, and ointments on the pharmacy shelf.

The best hope for sufferers is prevention. The following preventatives, used both before and after exposure to the plant's oil, work well: Prompt and proper cleansing of the skin within five minutes of exposure to urushiol can prevent a breakout. The most effective cleansing method is rinsing with plenty of cold, running water followed by a thorough swabbing with rubbing alcohol or Tecnu Poison Oak and Ivy Cleanser. Moist towelettes used on the trail to wipe skin that has contacted poison ivy, oak, or sumac can lessen the effects of a breakout. Washing with a mild, conditioning soap in warm water, however, is a bad choice, since warm water opens the skin's pores and the soap's oils can spread the urushiol around. Topical creams containing the drug bentoquatam (brand name Ivy Block) can also provide protection if applied before exposure. The cream works by creating a barrier on the skin.

♀
WOMAN-TO-WOMAN
POISON IVY

"Last spring, I wanted to buy some new insoles for my bike shoes. I went out to the garage to retrieve a mud-encrusted shoe, shaking my head at how lazy I'd been to leave them in that condition for several months. After much scrubbing, I bagged the shoe and headed off to the bike shop for the insoles. In the car on my way home, I remembered why I had been putting off cleaning them. My last ride had taken me through not only mud, but poison ivy. My carelessness resulted in a nasty breakout on my face, neck, arms, and legs. Needless to say, my husband got to clean the other shoe."

Barbara Mullins, teacher,
Kansas City, Missouri

Top: Western poison oak — west of Rockies, a shrub or vine where oak trees are found below 5,000 feet. Bottom: Poison oak — southeastern United States, usually found on sandy soil. (Illustrations show both summer and autumn foliage.)

BUGGED

"After a long day of trail riding, my friend and I were relaxing in front of a campfire and enjoying a bottle of red wine. Suddenly, she let out a yelp and shouted, 'There's a lizard crawling up my shorts!' and started dancing around the campfire. When we shone the flashlight on the ground, we saw that the "lizard" was actually only a walking stick (Pharnacia serratipes)."

Carolyn Schmidt, industry recruiter,
St. Louis, Missouri

Bugs

ANNOYING BITING BUGS Anyone who's been to summer camp or a company barbecue knows how crazy these bugs — including horseflies, mosquitoes, blackflies, chiggers, and gnats — can make you. In some parts of the country at certain times of the year, you may be better off just avoiding the woods rather than being feasted upon relentlessly. But there are steps you can take to lessen the swarms. Avoid wet, swampy areas where these bugs hang out. Use an insect repellent containing DEET (N, N-diethylmeta-toluamide). Sulfur powder sprinkled on your shoe tops and socks repels chiggers. Dabbing some witch hazel or an over-the-counter insect bite medication soothes any bites that you do get.

STINGING BUGS Usually, bees and wasps fall into the category of annoying bugs. Even if you get stung,

PREVENTING AND REMOVING TICKS

● Avoid trails that are heavily used by horses or pack animals.

● Wear light-colored clothing so ticks are easier to see and remove. Long sleeves and pants tend to keep ticks on your clothing, rather than on your skin.

● Use an insect repellent containing DEET or permethrin and apply as directed. DEET most effectively repels ticks when applied to clothing, rather than skin. However, DEET can damage synthetic fibers, making it unsuitable for use on some bike garments. Repellents containing permethrin should never be applied directly to the skin.

● Don't bring clothing that could contain ticks inside your tent or sleeping bag.

● Wash clothing worn in the outdoors in hot water and detergent as soon as possible upon your return home to prevent an infestation.

● After a ride, shower, then check yourself for ticks. An

you'll suffer only a quick bit of pain and maybe a little itchiness. Remove the stinger by gently scraping it with a knife edge. Soaking the area in a baking soda and water solution can reduce the itch.

However, if you are allergic to bee stings, they can be deadly. A severe allergic reaction can cause swelling of the tongue, nose, mouth, and esophagus; difficulty breathing; red, itchy hives; nausea; and vomiting. Treatment usually includes an injection of epinephrine (synthetic adrenaline) and antihistamine medication. If you are allergic to stings, always carry a treatment kit.

TICKS Approximately 10,000 cases of

the most common tick-related disease, Lyme disease, are diagnosed each year. Concentrated in the Northeast, northern Midwest, California, and Oregon, the disease has afflicted nearly 100,000 Americans since it was first discovered in Lyme, Connecticut in 1975. Cases have increased in the past 15 years by several thousand per year, with a high of 16,000 in 1996. All this may be enough to make outdoor

intimate friend can help you find ticks you may have missed.

● If you take your dog mountain biking in a tick-infested area, inspect him or her when you return. Remove ticks by hand or use a shampoo or dip containing an insecticide.

● If you find a tick attached to you, use tweezers to grasp the tick as close to your skin as possible, then firmly pull the tick away from the skin. Try not to crush the tick as you remove it. Once removed, kill the tick by placing it in rubbing alcohol or

cooking oil, burning it in a flame, or flushing it down the toilet. Clean the bite with alcohol and wash your hands with soap and hot water.

● Pick ticks that are crawling, but not yet attached to your skin, off by hand.

● Should you have a large number of ticks attached to your legs, some hardy souls say a quick lather with a pet flea and tick shampoo kills nearly all of them. I cannot vouch for the safety of this procedure, however.

Storm approaching, Utah's Slickrock Trail near Moab. Don't underestimate the power of rapidly moving summer thunderstorms; be prepared to take shelter.

encephalitis, paralysis of the facial muscles, abnormal heartbeat, numbness, and arthritic pain and swelling. Lyme disease can be diagnosed with a blood test (or with the appearance of the rash and flu-like symptoms) and is successfully treated with antibiotics that eliminate or reduce the severity of symptoms.

enthusiasts think twice about their safety in the woods.

But while ticks can carry disease, it is still unlikely that you'll get bitten by an infected tick and become ill. Ticks are usually harmless. I've removed hundreds and never gotten sick.

When a person is bitten by an infected tick, a red, ring-shaped rash usually, but not always, forms around the bite. Flu-like symptoms — headaches, fever, achy muscles, fatigue, and chills — generally coincide with the appearance of the rash. If left untreated, the disease will move into advanced stages, which can include meningitis,

A new Lyme disease vaccine awaiting approval by the U.S. Food and Drug Administration represents new hope for mountain bikers and other lovers of the outdoors. Smith-Kline Beecham's new LYMErix™ vaccine was approved by the FDA in December 1998 as a safe and effective way to prevent Lyme disease. The vaccine will be available in the Spring of 1999. It is not recommended for use by pregnant women, chronic arthritis sufferers, or people under age 15.

MAINTENANCE
AND
REPAIR

A mountain bike is built to be strong and durable to withstand rough trails. So you can just toss it in a corner of the garage after every ride and expect it to be ready for the next ride, right? Wrong. Just as with your car, if you neglect your mountain bike, you will suffer more breakdowns, more headaches, and less than perfect rides.

Take comfort in the fact that you'll never be as tough on equipment as the 200-pound guy who bombs down hillsides and torques his pedals with the force of Hercules. A woman's typically lighter weight and less aggressive riding style as compared to a man's means fewer break-downs and a longer life for her bike's frame and components. You may never "taco" a wheel or crack a crankarm. But, at some point, you will likely experience temperamental shifting, squeaky brakes, or a chain that hops off its cogs. And if you ride regularly, you will someday, inevitably, get a flat tire.

Mechanical endeavors are unfamiliar territory for many women. But I've learned that keeping a bike in good working order can be enlightening, satisfying, and empowering. The simple process of cleaning and lubing my bike has helped me know it better. Stripping the bike of its wheels, washing off accumulated

CYCLING CAREER

"I had always loved riding, so after college, I got a job in a bike shop just because I thought it would be fun. At the shop, I sold, assembled, and repaired bikes and pretty soon, I'd developed a big female customer base. After a while, I applied at Specialized. They hired me and now, three years later, I'm coordinating their pro mountain bike racing team. It's right up my alley. I love bikes and love that I can make my living with them. Bike companies are always looking for qualified women who know their stuff. It's a field where there are great opportunities for knowledgeable women."

Andrea Leininger, mountain bike race team coordinator, Morgan Hills California

mud, removing dirt from crevices, and lubricating moving parts requires you to look closely at the bike, bringing about a new understanding of how it works. For women whose mechanical knowledge and instincts have rarely been employed before, maintaining and repairing a bike is an eye-opening, confidence-building experience. With a little practice, you can keep your bike running well and be prepared for the occasional breakdown.

Learning About Your Bike

A good way to become intimately acquainted with your bike is to take a basic maintenance class. In the late autumn and winter, when business slows down, many bike shops offer maintenance courses. If your favorite shop is not offering classes, tell them you'd like to take one. Often, if enough customers express interest in a class, a shop will organize one. Another place to check for basic maintenance classes is through a local university extension service or "mini course" listing.

Community colleges and technical schools may also offer bike

RECOMMENDED READING

The following maintenance/repair manuals come highly recommended by bike mechanics and enthusiasts. They are technically complete, accurate, and easy for the layperson to follow. Invest in one or two for those cold winter evenings when there's nothing more satisfying than setting up the workstand, putting on a good CD, and giving your bike a little TLC.

● *Zinn and the Art of Mountain Bike Maintenance*, Lennard Zinn, Velo Press, 1998

● *Mountain Bike Maintenance*, Rob Van Der Plas, Bicycle Books, 1994

maintenance classes. And check in with your local bicycle club, as clubs sometimes hold maintenance clinics.

BASIC MAINTENANCE AND REPAIR

Some maintenance and repair tasks are quick and easy, while others are more time consuming and challenging and may be best left to the expert mechanic at the bike shop. Tasks worth knowing include fine-tuning the rear derailleur to ensure smooth shifting, adjusting the brakes to achieve optimal, noise-free stopping, repairing a broken chain to keep moving when you're 10 miles from civilization, and setting up suspension systems for the desired rate of compression and rebound. Check

Improving brake performance by adjusting the rear brake cable.

CLEANING AND LUBING THE BIKE

Some mountain bikers think of a dirty bike as proof that its rider must be a "real" off-roader who's not afraid of a little mud. But the fact is that a mud-encrusted bike with a gritty, dusty drivetrain is undependable. A clean bike with well-lubricated moving parts simply works better. Braking will be surer, shifting crisper, and suspension smoother. Your components will last longer, and

worn or defective parts will be easier to detect. Spend a little time giving your bike a bath after your next sloppy ride:

 ● Give the bike a quick rinse

continued on page 158

continued from page 157

with a gentle stream of water to loosen and soften dried mud. Avoid harsh car wash sprayers, as they can spray all the grease out of the bottom bracket, headset, or wheel hub bearings.

● Spray a degreasing solution like Pedro's, Finish Line, or Simple Green on the chain. Get a bucket of warm, soapy water (a tablespoon of dish or car washing soap works fine) and a scrub brush and clean the bike from top to bottom, frame, components, and all.

● Pay special attention to the drivetrain, scrubbing the chain, cogs, cassette, derailleurs, and pulleys. Use a small brush or long, pointed tool to get gunk from between the cogs while spinning the cranks. A chain cleaning device (manufactured by Finish Line, Park, and Bibox) filled with degreaser does a great job of getting all the grit and dust out of the chain links.

● Rinse the bike and dry it off with a clean towel. Drying your chain carefully prior to lubing protects it from rust.

● Lube it. Spray a synthetic bicycle lubricant such as TriFlow or Finish Line's Cross Country Lube on your chain and work it into the links by turning the cranks. Use a clean rag to wipe off the excess. Extra lube attracts dirt.

● If you want to make your bike's frame shine and sparkle like new, spray a little furniture polish or a bike frame polish on a clean, dry rag and wipe the frame. This treatment also repels dust and provides a bit of protection against rust.

out some of the excellent maintenance and repair manuals listed for in-depth directions on these and other valuable tasks.

Finding a Good Mechanic

As all of us who own cars know, finding and keeping a knowledgeable, helpful, fair mechanic is essential to keeping the car running. It's no different with your bike. The fact that we are females makes this task even more challenging. Some bike shop employees might assume that since we're female, we won't know the difference between a well-adjusted and poorly adjusted bike. Don't trust just any bike mechanic with your bike. Some shops hire young, inexperienced workers with little mechanical knowledge. Additionally, the rate of turnover at bike shops is frequently high; a shop that was reliable two years ago may not be so today.

Ask cycling enthusiasts you know which shops and mechanics they prefer. When you locate an experienced, trustworthy mechanic, ask for his or her services by name. Even if it takes a day or two longer, a good repair is worth waiting for. If you're not satisfied with work done on your bike, ask the manager to check the bike over for you. He or she should fix it to your satisfaction at no extra charge. Few managers at reputable shops will stand for shoddy workmanship.

The author checks the tension on the rear derailleur.

Periodically Replacing Parts

About once a year or every two years, your bike should have a complete overhaul with all the moving parts disassembled, cleaned, greased, and adjusted. This is a good time to replace worn parts, such as brake and shift cables, brake pads, the chain, and the tires. How quickly these parts wear out depends, of course, on how often you ride.

When squeezing the brake levers or shifting gears gets arduous, you may need to replace (or at least lubricate) your cables and cable housing. Unhook your brakes and look at your brake pads. If they

A sock makes a neat storage container for tools and repair kit.

appear worn and you can no longer see the grooves that improve stopping power, it's time to replace them. Can you see rust on your chain? Get a new one (make sure it's compatible with your drivetrain). Do the knobbies on your tires look chewed up or worn down? Replace those tires.

On-the-Trail Tool Kit

The following tools and supplies will get you through the most common on-trail mechanical problems and should be carried with

---

ASK THE EXPERT
ANGIE SHEEHY,
BIKE SALESPERSON,
St. Charles, Missouri

Q: Describe your job and how you got started.
A: I had been riding bikes and doing my own maintenance for years when I got the job in the bike shop. I started out assembling bikes and proved that I could do repairs. At one point, I was doing most of the repairs for our shop. I've moved into a semi-management and sales position now, and do repairs occasionally.
Q: How did you get into this line of work?
A: I love bikes — BMX, road, mountain, whatever — and I've always been mechanically inclined. I like knowing how things work. I

grew up working on my BMX bike because if I didn't, no one else would. My dad always did his own car maintenance and I liked to watch him. I'm weird. I like reading repair and owner's manuals and that, along with trial and error, is how I've learned bike repair. And I'm surrounded by mechanics at home. My husband is a boat mechanic and he and my son both like to work on cars.
Q: Are you ever at a disadvantage as a mechanic because of your sex?
A: Occasionally. But usually, it just takes some thought and innovation to overcome any strength limitations. Sometimes a bolt is seized or a tire is super tight on the rim, and I don't have enough hand or arm strength to remove it. So I get creative and look for ways to get addi-

you when you ride:
- Tire/tube patch kit (contains several patches, glue, and directions).
- Three tire levers.
- Allen wrenches in 3, 4, 5, and 6 mm sizes.
- Small adjustable wrench.
- Small flat-tip screwdriver.
- Chain repair tool.
- Small bottle of synthetic lubricant such as Tri-Flow or Finish Line Cross Country Lube.
- Frame pump.
- Spare inner tube.

FIXING A FLAT

Fixing a flat is easy, really easy. It's a task that everyone who rides should know. Why take the time and money to *drive* your bike to the bike shop and *pay* a mechanic to do what you could do yourself in five minutes? Why get stuck *walking* your bike five miles back to the trailhead, with darkness looming and kids waiting at the babysitter's, when you could have easily repaired that flat and ridden home in a third of the time?

To repair a flat tire, you'll need

tional leverage. I use "cheater bars" a lot (a length of pipe stuck on the end of a wrench for more leverage). If a bolt or seat post is corroded, I take a little extra time soaking it with penetrating oil to loosen it so it doesn't require as much raw power to remove. Lifting weights helps too. I have learned to rely on my own devices because if I ask the guys for help I hear, "Oh sure, let me help you, honey."

Q: What frustrations do you experience, being the only woman employee in your store?

A: I have to prove myself constantly, to both employees and customers. I'm suspect because I'm a woman. If someone doesn't know me, they assume I don't know anything about bikes. I've been at my shop for two years. I've been riding

and working on bikes for 15 years. I keep up-to-date on the latest technology by reading all the magazines, and still, guys with much less experience and knowledge question my abilities. Just the other day, I was talking about bikes with a guy I've known for a while and he said, incredulously, "Wow. You really do know your stuff." It takes a long time for even a qualified woman to get true respect in this industry.

Q: What joys do you experience working on bikes?

A: It's extremely satisfying work. I have a passion for it because bikes are my hobby as well as my job. Working on wheels is an art form. I like to true wheels; it's very relaxing. I'm looking forward to learning how to build nice wheels.

a patch kit, two or three tire levers, and a small tire pump. As mentioned earlier, always bring a spare inner tube of the correct size and type (Presta or Schraeder) because replacing an inner tube

ADJUSTING THE QUICK RELEASE

The quick release lever is a neat mechanism that allows you to remove and re-install your wheels with the flick of a lever; no wrenches or other tools are needed. But for all that they are convenient, failure to properly install and adjust wheels equipped with quick release levers can cause wheels to come off mid-ride, with an accident the probable result, and serious injury a real possibility. A surprising number of cyclists do not tighten the quick release nut properly. Here's how it's done.

Be sure to operate the quick release lever by hand only. Never use any other tool such as a hammer to tighten the lever, as it could cause damage.

ATTACHING THE WHEEL

① Move the quick release lever to the OPEN position and set the wheel so it firmly touches the interior of the fork end.

③ Turn the lever to the CLOSED position. The lever should be pointed toward the rear of the bike and positioned along the

② Move the quick-release lever to a position perpendicular to the bicycle frame (halfway between the opened and closed positions). Using your hand, turn the adjusting nut clockwise until it can no longer be turned.

is faster than repairing one.

Take the time to practice the following steps at home so that you feel comfortable when it happens on the trail. We'll cover the repair of a flat *rear* tire, since it is slightly

---

fork blade. Be sure to push the lever all the way to the closed position.

CAUTION: You cannot fasten the front wheel by twisting the quick release lever.

If the quick release lever can be easily pushed to the closed position, its clamping strength is insufficient. Return the lever to a position halfway between opened and closed (with the lever perpendicular to the bike frame), and again turn the adjusting nut clockwise to increase clamping strength. Push the quick release lever back to the closed position.

If the nut is so tight that the quick release lever cannot be pushed to the closed position, return it to the halfway position and turn the adjusting nut counter-clockwise to reduce the clamping strength.

REMOVING THE WHEEL
Move the quick release lever to the open position. This will release the wheel, and it can be

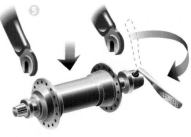

removed. There is no need to move the adjusting nut when removing the wheel.

BEFORE YOU RIDE
Check your quick release, making sure the lever is pushed fully to the closed position.

Lift up your bike so the front wheel is off the ground and give the top of the tire a sharp downward blow. The wheel should not come off or feel loose. This is only a quick check, and does not guarantee that the quick release lever has received adequate tightening torque. If uncertain, repeat the tightening process.

more complex than dealing with the front wheel.

① Unhook your brakes.

② Turn your bike upside down so it rests on the saddle and handlebars. Shift the chain until it is on the smallest cog on the rear cassette.

③ Open the quick release lever and unscrew the nut on the end of the skewer (axle) three or four turns.

④ Grasp the rear derailleur in one hand and twist it until it frees the chain and cogs. With the other hand, remove the wheel from the frame. If your wheel won't come out of the frame, try unscrewing the axle nut a few more turns, and jiggle the wheel as you remove it.

⑤ Find the valve along the wheel's rim. Remove the valve cap and depress the valve's needle to let all the air out of the inner tube. If there is a small locknut attached to the valve stem, unscrew and remove it. Be careful. The tiny valve cap and locknut are easy to misplace.

⑥ Using the unnotched side of a tire lever, work the lever between the edge of the tire and the wheel's rim until you can pry a bit of the tire off the rim. (Don't pry near the valve, as this could rip the tire.)

⑦ Secure the hooked end of the lever to a spoke. Take a second tire lever and repeat this process about six inches from the first lever. Insert the third lever between the tire and rim and gently run the lever around the rim edge until the tire zips off the rim.

Pull the damaged inner tube out of the tire, starting at the valve.

Carefully inspect the tire inside and out. If a sharp object like a thorn or tack has punctured your tube, it could still be stuck in the tire and can quickly flatten a newly installed tube unless you remove it.

Inflate the new inner tube just enough to give it shape. Starting with the valve stem, insert the tube into the tire, then pull the tire back up over the rim, either with your fingers or the tire levers. Make sure the tube is not pinched between the tire and rim.

Work the tire and tube until the tire is fully on the rim. Make sure the valve stem is straight, not bent sideways. Riding with the valve stem crooked could cause the tube to rip out. Inflate the tube to the recommended riding pressure. Screw the valve stem locknut back on.

Reinstall the wheel by again

grasping and twisting the rear derailleur and inserting the axle back into the "dropouts," or notches. Make sure the axle is fully seated in the dropouts or your wheel could fall out mid-ride. Reattach the brakes, making sure they don't rub on the tire, then tighten up the nut on the end of the quick release skewer (axle). Tighten until you feel tension against the quick release lever when you close it. Close the quick release lever. Check to see that the wheel spins freely, engage the brakes to make sure they contact the rims squarely, and you're ready to ride

The American Southwest presents some obvious maintence hazards.

S O U R C E S   &
R E S O U R C E S

After reading this book you may be ready to grab your bike — or head for the nearest bike store to buy a new one. If however, you seek company for your rides, or further information, we can get you started with the following list of organizations and publications to meet your needs.

ORGANIZATIONS

These leading organizations provide a wealth of information for new cyclists. You'll be able to choose one that has the right orientation for your interests.

ADVENTURE CYCLING ASSOCIATION

Box 8308
Missoula, MT 59807
1-800-755-2453
(406) 721-1776
www.adv-cycling.org.
Perhaps best known for its maps and networks of cross-country road bike routes, Adventure Cycling also develops mountain bike trails, including the Great Divide Trail stretching from Canada to Mexico along the Continental Divide. Publishes The Cyclists' Yellow Pages and a magazine.

BICYCLE FEDERATION OF AMERICA

1506 21st St. NW
Suite 200
Washington, D.C. 20036
(202) 463-6622
The Federation is a non-profit organization promoting bike use throughout the U.S. Primary source of information and statistics on U.S. bike use. Publishes a monthly newsletter.

HOSTELLING INTERNATIONAL-AMERICAN YOUTH HOSTELS

733 15th St. NW
Suite 840
Washington, D.C. 20005
(202) 783-6161
www.hiayh.org
Within the U.S., the organization operates more than 200 hostels (low-cost lodging) across the country and acts as a group tour organizer.

INTERNATIONAL MOUNTAIN BICYCLING ASSOCIATION

P.O. Box 7578
Boulder, Colorado
80306-7578
(303) 545-9011
imba@aol.com or
www.imba.com
IMBA promotes responsible riding and trail advocacy to keep trails across the U.S. open to mountain bikers.

LEAGUE OF AMERICAN BICYCLISTS

1612 K St. NW
Suite 401

Washington, D.C., 20006
(202) 8212-1333
www.bikeleague.org
LAB promotes government
support of bicycling as a trans-
portation alternative, provides
Effective Cycling classes to teach
proficient on-road cycling
techniques, and publishes a
magazine.

NATIONAL OFF-ROAD BICYCLING ASSOCIATION
1 Olympic Plaza
Colorado Springs
Colorado, 80909
(719) 578-4581
(888) 405-7223
NORBA is the national
governing body of mountain bike
racing the U.S.

RAILS-TO-TRAILS CONSERVANCY
1100 17th St. N.W.
10th Floor
Washington, D.C. 20036
(202) 331-9696
www.railtrails.org
The non-profit Conservancy
works to convert thousands of
miles of abandoned railroad
tracks in the U.S. to bike trails.

WOMEN'S MOUNTAIN BIKE TOURS, CLASSES, AND CLUBS
Perhaps you want some expert
instruction and hands-on
practice in mountain biking,
but would rather not do it in
front of the guys. Or maybe
you're looking for some female
company on rides or fancy a
vacation riding your bike with
other women. The following
organizations offer instruction in
the form of classes and camps,
off-road trips, and/or a network
of other women riders. Some
organizations, like WOMBATS,
offer all three.

TOUR ORGANIZERS
BACKROADS
801 Cedar St.
Berkeley, CA 94710
1-800-462-2848
www.backroads.com
While Backroads does not offer
women-only tours, they are one
of the largest bike touring com-
panies in the country and provide
off-road bike trips throughout the
U.S. and in exotic places like
Thailand and Bali.

ROADS LESS TRAVELED
2840 Wilderness Place
Suite F
Boulder, CO 80301
www.roadslesstraveled.com
This adventure touring company
provides fully-supported off-road
tours for women and/or men to
choice western mountain bike
locales.

RIM TOURS
1233 South Hwy. 191
Moab, UT 84532
(800) 626-7335
www.rimtours.com
In addition to its schedule of
fully-supported off-road tours in
Utah, Arizona, Colorado, and
Hawaii, Rim Tours can provide
custom tours for women.

WESTERN SPIRIT CYCLING
478 Maill Creek Rd.
Moab, UT 84532
(800) 845-2453
www.westernspirit.com
Tours for women and men in the
"slick rock" area of Utah and
beyond.

CLASSES
ADVENTUROUS WOMEN SPORTS
1378 De Haro St.
San Francisco, CA 94107
1-800-80WOMAN
www.adventurous.com
info@adventurous.com
Six-week women's mountain bike
course held in a state park near
San Rafael led by former national
champion racer Blair Lombardi.

ARTEMISIA ADVENTURES
1823 Bach Ave.
St. Louis, MO 63122
(314) 909-1903
Former pro mountain bike racer
and Eco Challenge vet Adrienne
Murphy leads one-day classes
and weekend adventures for
women with expert instruction,
gourmet food, and camraderie.

CORNELL OUTDOOR EDUCATION (CLASSES)
B01 Field House
Campus Rd.
Cornell University, Ithaca, NY
14853, (607) 255-6415
www.athletics.cornell.edu/coe
Instruction for women in a
supportive and fun environment.

ELK RIVER TOURING WOMEN'S SINGLE-TRACK CAMPS
Hwy. 219
Slatyfork, WV 26291
(304) 572-3771
The center of mountain biking in
West Virginia, Elk River Touring
Center offers women's and mixed
gender camps.

NANTAHALA OUTDOOR CENTER WOMEN'S CAMPS
13077 Hwy.
19 West
Bryson City, NC 28713
(888) 662-1662
(828) 488-2175
www.nocweb.com
Women-only or mixed classes
and camps in the beautiful
Smoky Mountains near
Asheville.

OUTDOOR EXPERIENCE MOUNTAIN BIKE ACADEMY
Catamount Outdoor Center
592 Governor Chittenden Rd.
Williston, VT 05495
(802) 879-6001
(802) 879-4960
www.together.net/catamont
The center offers mountain bike
skill clinics for women or mixed
groups weekly during the
summer.

WOMEN ON WHEELS
110 First St.
Elkins, WV 26241
(888) 311-BIKE
www.wvoutdoors.com/bike-works
A women's mountain bike weekend is offered twice a year and includes instruction on riding technique, maintenance, and nutrition and a guided excursion.

WEST COAST WOMEN'S CAMP
West Coast School of
Mountain Biking
P.O. Box 64160
Clarke Rd.
Coquitlam, British Columbia
Canada, V3J 7V6
(604) 931-6066
member.home.net/wcsmb
wcsmb@home.net
The school offers both multi-day and one-day skill classes for women on the challenging trails of British Columbia.

CLUBS
WOMEN'S MOUNTAIN BIKE AND TEA SOCIETY (WOMBATS)
P.O. Box 757
Fairfax, California 94978
(970) 247-0232
(415) 459-0980
www.wombats.org
Started by pro racer Jacquie Phelan, WOMBATS offers a wealth of information for women mountain bikers across the U.S., including a network of riders, group rides, and an annual jamboree in Durango, CO.

WOMEN'S RIDING NETWORK
1901 Ridge Lane
Pacific, MO 63069
(314) 271-7108 or
dirtgypsies@aol.com
The Women's Riding Network, started by Margo Carroll, provides a big list of Midwestern women riders, regular group rides, and a newsletter.

MAGAZINES
These established magazines can both thrill and lend assurance to those new to the sport. They are chock-full of techniques, recommendations, and usually ample back sections with advertisements for outfitters, organizations and products.

BICYCLING
135 North Sixth Street
Emmaus, PA, 18098
www.bicyclingmagazine.com
(610) 967-8722
800-666-2806
This is the nation's leading magazine on cycling, covering all aspects of the sport including road riding and touring.

BIKE
P.O. Box 1028
Dana Point, CA, 92629
(949) 496-5922
bikemag@petersenpub.com
With its innovative writing and stunning photography, Bike comes closest to capturing the feeling of mountain biking.

DIRT RAG
3483 Saxonburg Boulevard
Pittsburgh, PA, 15238
1-800-762-7617
(412)767-9910
www.dirtragmag.com
The "people's" mountain bike magazine, Dirt Rag provides an outlet for real mountain bikers and readers to contribute.

MOUNTAIN BIKE ACTION
25233 Anza Drive
Valencia, CA, 91355
(805) 295-1910
This magazine emphasizes the technical aspects of bikes and mountain biking with plenty of product reviews.

MOUNTAIN BIKE
33 East Minor Street
Emmaus, Pennsylvania, 18098
(610) 967-5171
800-666-1817
www.mountainbike.com

With its hip writing and graphics, Mountain Bike caters to a youthful, thrill-seeking mountain bike lifestyle and provides product reviews, trail information and racing news.

WOMEN'S WHEEL
Write Tracks, Inc.
P.O. Box 2073
Durango, CO, 81302
hulick@frontier.net
A quarterly newsletter for women who love to mountain bike.

VELONEWS
Inside Communications
1830 North 55th St.
Boulder, CO 80301
(303)440-0601
This is the racer's journal, covering the national and international scene for both road and mountain bike racing.

THE INTERNET
Any Internet search containing the keywords "mountain bike" will turn up hundreds of websites. Some offer valuable and interesting information, others don't. Following are a few of the best:

www.mtbr.com
This website's claim to fame is independent product reviews by individuals who own the equipment reviewed. The site also contains good information about places to ride, bike shops, books, and people to ride with.

www.gorp.com
The Great Outdoor Recreation Pages' mountain bike website offers loads of information about mountain biking locations, gear, books, and media. You can also "talk" with other mountain bikers and link to other cycling websites.

The Biker Girls' Forum offers women mountain bikers a great way to communicate electronically. You can meet other women in your area to ride with, share a secret trail, ask other women's opinions of a product you're considering, or just talk about how much you love mountain biking. Access the forum by conducting a search using the keywords "biker girls forum."

BOOKS

If you like to read or feel better easing slowly into this new venture, here are some suggestions. There are excellent guides for repairs and countless suggestions for making your outings more fun and comfortable.

FOR WOMEN ONLY

A Woman's Guide to Cycling, Susan Weaver, Ten Speed Press, 1998. This informative, easy-to-read book concentrates primarily on road cycling with a chapter on mountain biking. Helpful information for women with plenty of inspirational words from women cyclists.

MOUNTAIN BIKE BASICS AND MAINTENANCE

Mountain Bike: A Manual of Beginning to Advanced Technique, William Nealy, Menasha Ridge Press, 1992. The flip, cartoon-style approach to basic mountain bike technique may be visually jarring, but the information is sound and useful.
Mountain Bike Magazine's Complete Guide to Mountain Biking Skills, Rodale Press, 1996. Fun to read and full of essential tips for the beginning or intermediate mountain biker. Even advanced bikers will learn something.

Mountain Bike Maintenance, Rob van der Plas, Bicycle Books, 1994. Easy-to-follow illustrations and descriptions in a maintenance book dealing specifically with mountain bikes.

The New Complete Mountain Biker, Dennis Coello, Lyons and Burford, 1997. Great introductory book that includes hard-to-find information on off-road touring, a skill Coello has down pat.

Zinn and the Art of Mountain Bike Maintenance, Lennard Zinn, VeloPress, 1998. In this book, considered by many bike shop mechanics to be the essential maintenance manual for consumers, Zinn reveals his tips for keeping your mountain bike running smoothly.

URBAN CYCLING

Effective Cycling, John Forester, 1996, The MIT Press. At times tedious and dry, "Effective Cycling" is nonetheless the most complete source of time-tested on-road cycling techniques. Also contains interesting and surprising statistics on the safety of riding a bike on the road.

The Essential Bicycle Commuter, Trudy Bell, Ragged Mountain Press, 1998. Want to bike to work but still feeling a little unsure? Bell imparts helpful tips that only a longtime bike commuter could reveal.

Urban Bikers' Tricks and Tips: Low-Tech and No-Tech Ways to Find, Ride and Keep a Bicycle, Dave Glowacz, 1998, Wordspace Press. Glowacz, an Effective Cycling instructor and a city cyclist for 30 years, compiled this book of valuable suggestions and information from urban cyclists around the country.

VIDEOS

Our own Trailside® series of videos which aired on public television are perhaps the best inspiration we can offer to the novice mountain biker. Included are tips and techniques from experts and professionals. The following videos and others in the Trailside series may be purchased by calling 1-800-TRAILSIDE (1-800-872-4574). Catalog available.

Trailside's Mountain Biking in Utah. Experts teach the basics of gear, equipment, and technique riding the gnarly switchbacks of Moab. Includes behind-the-scenes footage and hints and tips. 45 minutes.
Trailside's Family Mountain Biking in South Dakota. Off-road family adventure in the rugged Black Hills of South Dakota; pedal through scenic meadows, watch free-roaming buffalo, and learn rough terrain biking skills. 45 minutes.

A SAMPLING OF OTHER VIDEOS

Battle at Durango: The First Ever Mountain Bike World Championships. An inside look at the big race with equal time given to male and female racers. 60 minutes. New & Unique Videos, 7323 Rondel Ct., San Diego, CA 92119, 1-800-365-8433, www.newuniquevideos.com

Full Cycle: A World Odyssey. Follow a couple on their adventurous around the world off-road bike tour. 107 minutes. New & Unique Videos, 7323 Rondel Ct., San Diego, CA 92119, 1-800-365-8433, www.newuniquevideos.com

Fundamentals of Bicycle Maintenance. REI mechanics explain the basics for mountain and road bikes. 55 minutes. Elliott Bay Film Company, (206) 784-4666 or Backcountry Bookstore (206) 290-7652.

Great Mountain Biking Video.
An introduction to the sport;
perfect for true beginners. 50
minutes. New & Unique Videos,
7323 Rondel Ct., San Diego,
CA 92119, 1-800-365-8433,
www.newuniquevideos.com
*Mountain Bike Anatomy:
Assembly, Care, and Upgrades.*
How to take care of your bike.
60 minutes. New & Unique
Videos, 7323 Rondel Ct.,
San Diego, CA 92119,
1-800-365-8433,
www.newuniquevideos.com

Ultimate Mountain Biking.
Technique instruction for intermediate to advanced mountain
bikers and racers. 61 minutes.
New & Unique Videos, 7323
Rondel Ct., San Diego, CA
92119, 1-800-365-8433,
www.newuniquevideos.com

CLOTHING AND ACCESSORIES FOR WOMEN

While specialized clothing for
cycling is not a requirement (you
can have a fun ride in a t-shirt
and shorts), it can make the experience much more comfortable.
Luckily, a number of companies
now offer padded cycling shorts,
jerseys, tights, gloves, shoes,
helmets, and even sunglasses
designed with women in mind. If
your local bike shop doesn't stock
a particular company's offerings,
ask if they can order them.

ANDIAMO, (CLOTHING)
P.O. Box 1657
Sun Valley, ID 83353
(208) 726-1385
1-800-333-6141

BELL SPORTS, (HELMETS)
Attn: Customer Service,
Route 136 East,
Rantoul, IL 61866
1-800-456-BELL,
www.bellsports.com

BELLWETHER, (CLOTHING)
375 Alabama St.
San Francisco, CA 94110,
(415) 863-0436
1-800-321-6198
www/bellwethersf.com

CANNONDALE, (CLOTHING)
16 Trowbridge Dr.
Bethel, CT 06801
1-800-726-2453
www. cannondale.com

**CRASH PADS,
(PROTECTIVE PADS)**
2625 Southeast 39th Loop
Unit C
Hillsboro, OR, 97123
1-800-964-5993
www.crash-pads.com

CRATONI, (HELMETS)
3550 North Union Dr.
Olney, IL 62450
(618) 393-2955
800-507-6444

DIADORA, (CLOTHING)
distributed by
Gita Sporting Goods, Ltd.
12600 Steel Creek Rd.
Charlotte, NC 28273
1-800-SAY-GITA

DIRT DESIGNS, (CLOTHING)
2805 Wilderness Pl. #1200
Boulder, CO 80301
(303) 541-0662
1-800-269-6641
www.dirtdesigns.com

GIRO SPORT DESIGN, (HELMETS)
380 Encinal St.
Santa Cruz, CA 95060
(408) 457-4476
1-800-969-4476
www.giro.com

GRANDOE, (CLOTHING)
74 Bleecker St.
Gloversville, NY 12078
1-800-472-6363

KOULIUS ZAARD, (CLOTHING)
2682 Middlefield Rd.
Unit K
Redwood City, CA 94063
(415) 364-9575
1-800-KOULIUS
www.kzaard.com

LAKE, (SHOES)
P.O. Box 5490
Evanston, IL 60204
1-800-804-7777
www.lakeshoes.com

**MT. BORAH DESIGNS,
(CLOTHING)**
P.O. Box 518
Coon Valley, WI 54623
(608) 452-2138
1-800-354-2825
www.mtborah.com

PEARL IZUMI, (CLOTHING)
620 Compton Ave.
Broomfield, CO 80020
1-800-328-8488
www.pearlizumi.com

SHEBEEST, (CLOTHING)
2106 Ladrillo Ave.
Irvine, CA 92606
(949) 733-9992
www.shebeest.com

SHIMANO, (SHOES)
1 Shimano Dr.
Irvine, CA 92618
1-800-353-3817
www.shimano.com

SMITH, (SUNGLASSES)
P.O. Box 2999
Ketchum, ID 83340
1-800-459-4903
www.smithsport.com

SPORTOBIN, (CLOTHING)
P.O. Box 115
Hull, MA 02045
(781) 925-5339
1-800-424-3843
www.sportobin.com

SUGOI, (CLOTHING)
144 East 7th Ave.
Vancouver, BC V5T 1M6
1-800-432-1335
www.sugoi.com

SWOBO, (CLOTHING)
330 Townsend #16
San Francisco, CA 94107
1-800-SWOBO-4-U
www.swobo.com

ZEAL, (SUNGLASSES)
59 South Main
Suite 143
Moab, UT 84532
(435) 259-6970
1-888-454-9325
www.zealmaniak.com

ZOIC, (CLOTHING)
2415 3rd. St.
Suite 230
San Francisco, CA 94107
(800) 241-WEAR
www.zoic.com

MAIL-ORDER SOURCES OF CLOTHING AND ACCESSORIES

Ordering clothing and equipment from catalogs is standard procedure for some cyclists, especially those who might not live within shouting distance of a well-stocked bike shop. Some mail-order companies now even cater specifically to women.

ATHLETA
1610 Corporate Circle
Petaluma, CA 94954
888-322-5515
www.athleta.com
Athleta offers women's clothing for cycling, hiking, running, and other active pursuits.

BIKE NASHBAR
4111 Simon Rd.
Youngstown, OH 44512
1-800-NASHBAR
www.bikenashbar.com

COLORADO CYCLIST, INC.
3970 E. Bijou St.
Colorado Springs, CO 80909
1-800-688-8600
www.coloradocyclist.com

EXCEL SPORTS BOULDER
2045 32nd St.
Boulder, CO 80301
1-800-627-6664
www.excelsports.com

PERFORMANCE BICYCLE SHOP
P.O. Box AW
Beckley, WV 25802
1-800-727-2453
www.performancebike.com

REI
1700 45th St. East
Sumner, WA 98390
1-800-426-4840
www.rei.com,
www.rei-outlet.com

TERRY PRECISION CYCLING FOR WOMEN,
1704 Wayneport Rd.
Macedon, NY 14502
1-800-289-8379
www.terrybicycles.com

TITLE NINE SPORTS
5743 Landregan St.
Emoryville, CA 9460,
(510) 655-5999
1-800-609-0092
www.title9sports.com
Title Nine Sports sells women's active wear, including cycling clothing.

BIKES FOR WOMEN

The following companies — some major manufacturers and some small, independent builders — offer quality mountain bikes and/or components that are especially suited to women. Flip through the pages of their catalogs and you'll find some bikes with lighter, proportionally-smaller frames, shorter top tubes, shorter stems, narrower handlebars, short reach brake levers, and custom bike options, along with other goodies.

AMP RESEARCH
23531 Ridge Route
Laguna Hills, CA 92563
1-888-983-2209
(949)461-5990
www.amp-research.com

BARRACUDA
51 Executive Blvd.
Farmingdale, NY 11735
1-800-338-7677

CANNONDALE
16 Trowbridge Dr.
Bethel, CT 06801
1-800-BIKEUSA
www.cannondale.com

GT BICYCLES
2001 East Dyer Rd.
Santa Ana, CA 92705
1-800-743-3248
www.gtbicycles.com

INDEPENDENT FABRICATIONS
P.O. Box 98
Summerville, MA 02143
(617) 666-3609
www.ifbikes.com

JAMIS
151 Ludlow Ave.
Northvale, NJ 07647
1-800-222-0570
www.jamisbikes.com

KONA
2455 Salashan
Ferndale, WA 98248
(360) 366-0951
www.konaworld.com

LITESPEED TITANIUM
P.O. Box 22666
Chattanooga, TN 37422
(423) 238-5530
www.litespeed.com

MARIN
84 Galli Dr.
Novato, CA 94949
1-800-222-7557
www.marinbikes.com

TERRY PRECISION CYCLING FOR WOMEN
1704 Wayneport Rd.
Macedon, NY 14502
1-800-289-8379
www.terrybicycles.com

TREK
801 West Madison St.
Waterloo, WI 53594
1-800-369-8735
www.trekbikes.com.

P H O T O
C R E D I T S

BOB ALLEN: 6, 78, 81, 86
DUGALD BREMNER: 73
SKIP BROWN: 27, 76, 101
DENNIS COELLO: 8, 12, 13, 14, 17 (all), 25, 30, 31, 33, 42, 43 (top), 46, 51 (top), 52,
53 (both), 56, 58, 60, 63, 64, 66, 69, 70, 71 (top), 72, 82, 84, 87, 88 (both), 89, 90 (both),
91, 92, 93, 94, 95, 96, 97, 99, 102, 103, 105, 106, 107, 108, 111, 112, 117, 119,
212 (both, 122, 125, 126, 127, 129, 130, 131, 133, 134, 136, 138, 141, 143, 144, 145,
149, 154, 157 (top), 159, 160, 164 (all), 165 (all), 166
CARL GOODING: 29 (left), 32, 51 (bottom), 71 (bottom)
JOHN GOODMAN: 11, 18, 19, 29 (right), 34, 36, 38, 39, 40 (all), 41, 43 (bottom), 44 (all),
45, 47, 49, 50, 55, 57 (all), 67 (both), 113, 124, 155
MICHAEL SHAW: 157 (bottom)

INDEX

pumps, 45, 80
punctures, protection against, 45

Q

quadriceps, exercises for, 115, 116
quick-release flange, 79, 162-63

R

races, 100
racks, 47-48, 53, 54
rain gear, 69, 72, 133
reach, and bike fit, 25-28
rear lights, 51
rear-view mirrors, 53
reflectors, 51-52
repair, see maintenance
resources, 74, 167-72
rim brakes, 29, 30
rooftop car racks, 54
Rules of the Trail (IMBA), 96

S

saddlebags, 49
saddles, 39-42
    bike fit and, 26, 27
    choosing, 41-42
    comfort issues for, 40-41, 145-47
    cutout, 41
    height of, 17, 83
    locking of, 47
    position of, 41
    seat fore/aft, 26
    soft gel, 42
    under-seat packs for, 48, 50
safety, 139-45
    animals and, 140-45
    first aid and, 142
    flags for, 108
    helmets for, 55-57
    in hunting season, 145
    in traffic, 134, 137
    when riding alone, 106-7, 140
Schraeder valves, 44, 45
screwdrivers, 46, 80
seat fore/aft, 26
seat packs, 48, 50
seat posts, 37, 47, 83
security, locks for, 47
shades (sunglasses), 71-72
shifters, 30, 33-34, 78
shifting gears, 77-79
    before descents, 88
    pedaling while, 78
shirts, 64-66
shock absorption, 22, 23, 34-35, 37, 146
shoes, 31-33, 67-68
shorts, 40, 59-62, 146
shouldering your bike, 88
shoulder pain, 147
single-track riding, 75-77, 78
skidding, 81
skirts and skorts, 134
snacks, 128

snakes, 143-45
soft surfaces, biking on, 92
solo, riding, 105-7, 140
spine, stretching exercises for, 115-16
sports drinks, 120
standover clearance, 25
steel frames, 21-22
stems, 27-28, 48, 77
step-through frames, 22
strength training, 115-18
stretching exercises, 115-16
sunglasses, 71-72
sunscreen, 124, 125
suspension, 34-38
    dual, 35-36
    front, 23, 34-35
    full, 21, 35-38
    for single-track riding, 75
suspension forks, 23, 27, 34-35, 48, 146
suspension seat posts, 37
suspension stems, 48

T

target heart rate, 114
test rides, 12, 26
theft, prevention of, 47
thermoplastic frames, 23
ticks, 152-54
tights, 63
tire irons, 80
tires, 43-45
    fixing flats, 161-66
    inflation of, 79
    liners for, 45
    patch kits for, 45, 80
    pre-ride check of, 79
    replacement of, 160
    tread patterns, 44
    underinflated, 45
    width of, 44
titanium frames, 24
toe clips, 31-32
tools, 45-46, 80, 160-61
topographical (topo) maps, 99
tops, 64-66
tours, 100, 168
traffic, bike safety and, 134, 137
trailers, children in, 108
trail riding, 93-112
    finding sites for, 95, 97-100
    IMBA's rules for, 96
    minimizing damage in, 98
    navigation for, 97-100
    partners for, 101-12
trigger shifters, 33-34
tubes, 21, 24
    alterations to, 26
    butted, 22
    frame geometry and, 31-32
    horizontal top, 22
    reach and, 25, 26, 27
    sloping top, 22
tubes, tire, 44-45, 80

turning, 81-82
twist shifters, 33-34

U

underpants, 60-61
under-seat wedge packs, 48, 50
urban riding, 129-38
    clothing tips for, 133-34
    harassment in, 131
    helmet and hair in, 135
    modified bike for, 131
    public transit and, 136
    tips for, 137
    workplace showers in, 132-33
U-style locks, 47

V

valve stems, 44-45
V-brakes (direct-pull brakes), 29, 81
videos, 74, 170-71

W

water, 80, 118-20
    for dog, 111
    for first aid, 142
    natural sources of, 119-20
    tips about, 119-20
water bottles, 42-43
weight:
    bike cost and, 18-19, 37
    diet for control of, 126-28
    distribution of, 32
    of frame, 21
    of men vs. women, 20
    of titanium bikes, 24
weight-bearing exercises, 118
wheels, 28-29
    attachment of, 162-63
    extra set of, 132
    pre-ride check of, 79-80, 163
    quick-release lever on, 79, 162-63
    removal of, 163
    skidding of, 81
    tracking of, 37
    valve stems and, 44-45
whistles, police-style, 54
wild animals, 143
WOMBATS (Women's Mountain Bike and Tea Society), 99
women:
    bike fit for, 24-28
    larger, clothing for, 64
    lightweight bikes for, 21
    men's proportions vs., 26, 27
    networks for, 99, 101
    as riding partners, 101-3
    upper-body strength of, 20, 117
    weight of men vs., 20
wrenches, 45, 46, 80
wrists, numbness in, 146

Y

yeast infections, 61, 146
yoga, 114